Singapore's Success

ENGINEERING ECONOMIC GROWTH

Singapore's Success

ENGINEERING ECONOMIC GROWTH

Henri Ghesquiere

THOMSON

Australia • Canada • Mexico • Singapore • Spain • United Kingdom • United States

THOMSON™

Singapore's Success: Engineering Economic Growth
by Henri Ghesquiere

For more information, please contact:
Thomson Learning
(a division of Thomson Asia Pte Ltd)
5 Shenton Way
#01-01 UIC Building
Singapore 068808

Or visit our Internet site at http://www.thomsonlearningasia.com

Thomson Learning offices in Asia: Bangkok, Beijing, Hong Kong, Kuala Lumpur, Manila, Seoul, Singapore, Taipei, Tokyo.

Printed in Singapore
1 2 3 4 5 SLP 09 08 07 06

ISBN-13: 978-981-4195-28-7
ISBN-10: 981-4195-28-6

To Mieke

Contents

Preface

The promised island

January 5, 2004. In what seemed but minutes after touching down at Changi Airport, my luggage appeared and was handed to a solicitous taxi driver. As we navigated the lanes of gleaming new cars in air-conditioned comfort, rows of manicured flowering bushes extended their endless tropical welcome among lush greenery and glimpses of the sea. In the distance lay the world's busiest container port. Closer by, Singapore's inviting glass and steel skyline opened up, home to over 6,000 multinational corporations, just when dapper young professionals went on their lunch break in this urbane multi-ethnic society. This was the first day of my final two-year assignment on the staff of the International Monetary Fund. After 25 years of service in numerous, mainly low-income, countries, this place looked like the *Promised Land.*

Promised by whom? Perhaps by my IMF supervisors as recompense for the hardships of oxygen-deprived La Paz, sand-swept Nouakchott, or blistering cold Kyiv? Hardly. Each of those earlier assignments offered their own rewards, not least a profound professional satisfaction from working with dedicated government officials toward improving their struggling economies.

No, a destination held out by my colleagues in the international development community and I during those 25 years. Underlying the policy recommendations that we offered was the basic premise: implement the right economic policies—consistently—and your country will harvest high economic growth and an end to absolute poverty. Our policy advice, even if painful, always envisaged the eventual attainment of each economy's potential: decent and affordable housing for all in clean surroundings, quality healthcare and education, fulfilling employment and the chance for one's children to advance in life—as modern Singapore has done. This city-state, as proclaimed by its first Prime Minister Lee Kuan Yew had "progressed from a Third World country to a First World nation in one generation" (Lee, 2000).

Instilling the specifics of good economic policy was the purpose of my stay in Singapore. During the two years I served as Director of the IMF-Singapore Regional Training Institute (STI), a joint undertaking between the Government of Singapore and the IMF, close to 2,000 government and central bank officials from the Asia-Pacific region would visit Singapore for one- to three-week courses. Participants, hailing from Afghanistan to Tonga, and some 40 countries in between, came to study how macroeconomic policies and sound principles of finance could help achieve sustained economic growth. For several of them, this was the first trip outside their home country. Driving through this ultra-clean and modern city, many no doubt wondered about the seemingly secret key to unlocking the potential of their own societies.

Finding that key is the quest behind this book: what explains Singapore's remarkable economic growth? No other economy grew faster during the 40-year period ending in 2000. What lessons might Singapore's experience hold for other countries, developing and advanced alike? Visitors to this small city-state tend to be amazed at the state-of-the-art transportation and high-rise glitz. But many, including from developed countries, upon learning about Singapore's economic policies and institutions, are no less surprised at this invisible architecture.

Acknowledgments

The extent of my indebtedness is evident from the footnotes and bibliography. Reproduction of several diagrams from David Weil's excellent textbook is gratefully acknowledged. Many have read the manuscript, provided corrections, and offered numerous perceptive comments that have enriched the final version. My genuine thanks to

Luc De Wulf, Anita Doraisami, Joshua Greene, Khor Hoe Ee, Jerome La Pittus, Lim Chong Yah, David Orsmond, Euston Quah, Leo Van Houtven, and Peter Wilson. The blend of frankness and encouragement that marked their reviews is deeply appreciated. Ernesto Zedillo, former President of Mexico and now in a leading position at Yale University, took time from his exacting schedule to read the book. Elizabeth Daniel skillfully edited the manuscript into a polished product. Working as a team with her, and Thomson Learning's Paul Tan and Pauline Lim has been a delight.

Many of the insights that underlie this volume were acquired during my 27 years with the IMF. Former colleagues and supervisors taught me a lot, as did country officials and others with whom I worked closely, including staff from the World Bank. In writing this book, I had the outsider's advantage of noticing what is strikingly unusual about Singapore. But I needed to learn a lot quickly. The insights provided in the writings of, among others, Professors Gavin Peebles, Peter Wilson, Lim Chong Yah, Linda Low, Diane Mauzy, and R.S. Milne, and of IMF staff who worked on Singapore over the years, proved particularly valuable. But I must emphasize that the views in this book are strictly my own and not of any organization I have been, or am currently, associated with. Remaining errors of facts, interpretation, or judgment are solely mine.

My first book *Between Eden and Utopia—Development in Southeast Asia* was published in 1976. It was dedicated to the young people of the region, for whom development meant a unique challenge of leadership and talent. *Singapore's Success* is dedicated to Mieke, my wife, in gratitude for standing by me throughout. Without her, this book, as much else in our lives, would have stayed an unformed concept.

Introduction

CAN SINGAPORE'S SUCCESS BE TRANSFERRED ELSEWHERE?

Singapore's success, some experts say, cannot be replicated. The country has unique advantages. The concentration of its 4.3 million people on an island with an area of less than 40km by 20km facilitates cost-effective delivery of social services, infrastructure, and governance in ways that are not available to continent-size countries such as India or Brazil. Unlike metropolises elsewhere, Singapore's sovereign-nation status gives it control of immigration from its hinterland. The natural deep-water port and strategic location gave it a head start in international trade and exchange that landlocked countries such as Nepal can only dream of. And what could countries such as Cambodia, where traditional agriculture still predominates, learn from an economy whose primary sector has shrunk to orchid-growing and fish-farming, miniscule in the overall economic picture?

Yet other countries have learned from Singapore. China's momentous decision in 1978 to reverse five centuries of economic isolation was influenced in part by Deng Xiaoping's visit to Singapore that year. His dream to "plant a thousand Singapores in China" sparked numerous delegations on study tours to the island. South Korea was impressed with Singapore's success in overcoming corruption. The city-state's mastery in keeping urban traffic flowing has fascinated officials from many countries, and its housing program is studied by planners from around the world. Dubai eyes Singapore continually. Singapore's welcoming of multinational corporations (MNCs), with generous incentives and a one-stop window—at a time when other countries shunned them—has since found numerous followers. Export-oriented industrialization strategies have also become common. During a 1970 visit to the Istana, Singapore's presidential residence, Malaysia's former Prime Minister Dr Mahathir Mohamad, expressed keen interest in how the sprawling grounds were kept so green. Diplomatic courtesy no doubt inspired visiting dignitaries to express niceties, but imitation often followed flattery.

Countries, large and small, can learn from each other. Nineteenth-century Germany learned from England's industrial revolution; Japan after the Meiji Restoration in 1867–68 was impressed with Germany's economic catching up; Singapore was inspired by Japan's success; and the British Labor Party recently made a visit to study Singapore's healthcare system, completing the circle. Learning does not entail transplanting successful policies uncritically into foreign soil. Literally copying another country's template is of limited use and can even harm. As a minimum, however, countries or their individual enterprises derive inspiration from others. This book tries to distinguish between general principles that have wider applicability and their specific implementation in the Singapore context. How has Singapore, in its particular circumstances, implemented these basic principles? Moreover, if Singapore's experience corroborates the validity of these fundamentals, other countries, developing and advanced, might benefit from exploring how they in turn can adapt these basics to their own specific environment. Lessons can be drawn without elevating Singapore as a "model" to be copied.

SHOULD SINGAPORE'S STRATEGY BE EMULATED?

Even admirers of Singapore's economic performance point to imperfections. However impressive, the country's development policies, they aver, have technical flaws that other countries may wish to avoid. Singapore is one of only a handful of countries where International Monetary Fund (IMF) staff has questioned whether government saving might not be excessive, that is, favoring consumption by future generations at the expense of the current one.[1] With regard to Singapore's economic development record, the

1 International Monetary Fund (2005), p.15.

proverbial glass may be 85 percent full, but critics tend to focus on the 15 percent that is empty. Noted academics have expressed concern about Singapore's Central Provident Fund (CPF), an individual mandatory savings scheme originally meant as retirement income. In their view, the subsequent reorientation of the scheme to finance widespread home ownership has resulted in insufficient liquid savings and an inadequate prospective income stream for many retirees. Others have stressed that the dominant role of public enterprises and government guidance in the economy may have stymied innovative local private entrepreneurship, a key driver of growth in mature economies such as Singapore. Observers also bemoan the emphasis placed on written examinations in the centuries-old mandarin tradition, which they claim has dulled creativity in education.

Policy shortcomings in Singapore's context can perhaps be viewed as new challenges that inevitably arise as circumstances evolve. Deficiencies flag the need for ongoing redefinition of strategy. Governments cannot address all issues at once and must approach them sequentially. In fact, the Singapore government tinkers, almost obsessively, with its development strategy to cope with new challenges to its competitive position as soon as they emerge on the distant horizon. Yesterday's virtue can become tomorrow's obstacle. Pragmatic policy change then solves the problem…unless the required lead time is too long—it takes a loaded tanker several miles of seaway to change its course. Can teachers become comfortable overnight with the reality that a question may have more than one good answer?

In this book, we consider the timing and sequencing of Singapore's policies and their evolution over time. As to the 85 percent of the glass, it offers other countries a compelling drink for thought.

SINGAPORE'S ECONOMIC SUCCESS—AT TOO HIGH A COST?

Naysayers are of the view that Singapore's experience should not be emulated, but for a different reason: the values that helped define the country's development strategy conflict with the preferences of other societies—and of some Singaporeans as well. Many outside the country lament capital punishment for crimes such as drug trafficking or homicide. They also resent the paternalism of public education campaigns and control that the government exerts over political activity. In their view, the state—and not individuals or their families—should assume financial responsibility for the unemployed and aging. Constraints on press freedom are protested. Labor unions should be maintained at arm's length from the government. Many are uncomfortable with the means the government employs to help it achieve what they consider to be a de facto one-party democracy. Official prickliness at dissent has spawned a culture that has been characterized as "sterile," even though Singapore has become more open and vibrant.

Yet, as to the ultimate outcome of what democratic societies hope to achieve, Singapore scores high. Property rights are secure. Individuals are protected from predation by the state, its officers, and fellow humans. The crime rate is low while public-sector integrity is high. The quest for unearned advantage or privilege based on favor or position is limited. Individuals are provided the means to be upwardly mobile. Gender equality is average relative to global standards. Meritocracy governs recruitment and promotion. Taxation is low compared to countries with similar income levels. Ethnic, religious, and racial discrimination are condemned de jure and minimized de facto, though possibly not completely eliminated. The government follows publicly known rules—of its own making, cynics will add—and it submits to periodic elections, which it knows it will win, albeit not by how much, realists will counter.

Herein lies the rub. Singapore's development strategy has been supported by political stability. This orderliness has been achieved within the framework of a democracy that has been dominated by a single political party—the People's Action Party (PAP), in power since 1959. Periodic multi-party elections take place and freedom of expression and dissent are condoned, albeit within limits meant to maintain a strong government capable of forging a consensus on sound policies. To Westerners, who are steeped in a tradition of dissent that overcame the absolute power of monarchs, self-determination and expression by freely forming groups within society are deeply cherished values. In the Chinese tradition—to which 78 percent of Singaporeans relate—where the state historically defined doctrine, exerted control, and expected obedience in exchange for providing order, the costs and benefits of one-party domination are weighed differently, not only by the leaders, but on available evidence, by a majority of the people as well.

Is there a tradeoff between economic performance and liberal democracy? The governing elite believes so. In its view, "soft authoritarianism" and collective self-discipline have contributed to strong economic performance and rapid catch-up with the West, which unfettered liberal democracy, in Singapore's particular historical circumstances, would not have made possible. The main theme of this book is that economic outcomes, policies, economic and political institutions, attitudes, values, and leadership in Singapore are closely interwoven. Their exceptionally strong internal coherence and mutual reinforcement, over a long period of time, account for the impressive results obtained. It is this coherence of strategy that the PAP has protected, some would say obsessively.

Other societies would have struck the balance differently. Singapore's younger generation may yet do so. As Singapore catches up to advanced-country income levels, it is increasingly being measured against standards of openness that prevail elsewhere. For sure, Singaporeans feel entitled to decide for themselves the speed and direction in which they wish to shape their society. But the values and aspirations of Singaporeans, in particular the younger generation, will likely change, along with increased affluence and education. The remarkable economic uplifting against the odds that occurred in their grandparents' tumultuous time will fade into what they have shelved as ancient history. In their view, a less restricted civil society and enduring social order can coexist in 21st-century Singapore. Besides, the imperatives of innovativeness and creativity on which a maturing economy draws for continued economic growth, will impose their own requirements for increased openness.

More openly contentious public debate could strengthen Singapore. The government has been suspicious that increased disclosure of its finances or the opportunism of an unfettered press is likely to erode its lifetime work of educating the people to the virtues of discipline and enlightened policies. Yet, Singapore's record of extraordinary economic ascent, while nurturing social harmony and building a fiscal position that can comfortably confront looming financial challenges better than any other rapidly aging society without the benefit of an oil export windfall, attests to the wisdom of its leaders. Singaporeans, even younger ones, are aware of their economy's vulnerability to intensifying global competition and of the need for sound financial policies. Like many a parent of maturing adolescents, the government might yet be pleasantly surprised at the responsibility with which the public handles additional disclosure of its finances and greater openness more generally.

Engineering prosperity

Engineering prosperity is at the heart of Singapore. I do not make this statement lightly. It does not ignore the aspirations of the Malay, Indian, and Chinese communities that make up Singapore or the fullness of their different cultures and heritage, neither do I denigrate the spiritual, cultural, or plain human values of Singaporean families. Nonetheless, consistently creating prosperity is the public persona that Singapore, as a society, projects to the outside world.

Here the theme of the economy dominates. Striving collectively to achieve prosperity galvanizes the energy of Singaporeans, more than is the case with other societies. Some in Singapore might object to my highlighting the mercantile motive. After all, great efforts have been devoted with remarkable success to building national cohesion and instilling a sense of civic duty and service. Progress in the theater, music, and the arts has been impressive. This book does not reduce all that Singapore stands for to a common monetary denominator. Instead, the view I suggest is that the overarching emphasis on achieving sustained prosperity has itself provided a powerful rationale for nation-building and other development ideals. The Singapore authorities have preached the secular religion of public pursuit of prosperity for all. The path to this nirvana ran through export-led industrialization by inviting MNCs to locate in Singapore. This necessitated political and social stability, which in turn required ethnic and religious harmony and sharing benefits by providing equal opportunity. Judicious policies created incentives and opportunities for superior performance, allowing Singapore's elite and the population at large to prevail and thrive.

Engineering is central to Singapore. Not only as one of the first high-tech electronic societies that were wired into the rest of the world, but also as applied to economic strategy and even molding society.[2] The political elite's passionate pursuit of shared prosperity required assembling together many diverse components, of policies, institutions, attitudes, and political savvy, to create an intricate and highly effective mechanism that, moreover, required constant upgrading. The discipline inherent in work ethic and delayed gratification of postponing consumption, exposure to market competition, meritocracy in schooling and civil service, public integrity, and law and order have all served as essential lubricants. This strategy is an enlightened one: existing doctrines and precepts on development policies, institutions, and political economy of implementation were rationally examined for their merit and pragmatically adopted, adapted, and pursued to their logical consequences, in light of Singapore's circumstances and the actual results obtained.

2 In 2005, The World Economic Forum's *Global Information Technology* report ranked Singapore first among 115 countries for making use of Information and Communication Technology developments. See http://www.wereform.org/site/homepublic.nsf/content.

Is Singapore's success unique?

Some may point out that Singapore's success is not unique. A small number of other economies, including Japan and its former colonies Taiwan and South Korea, have achieved results that are no less remarkable. The performances of Malaysia, Chile, Botswana, and others, not to mention China and India, merit detailed study as well. That view is unobjectionable. In fact, a pioneering World Bank study in 1993 on the "East Asian Miracle" demonstrated how several successful countries adopted a few basic principles in sometimes quite different forms. Countries that have sustained high growth have adopted different approaches. Income convergence does not require convergence of specific policies and institutions. The art of formulating effective growth strategies, as stressed by the World Bank, lies in careful consideration of country-specific factors, opportunities, and constraints, not least in the political sphere. There is no unique way to succeed.[3] Singapore is only one case history.

The structure of the book

Chapter 1 depicts Singapore's development record and decomposes the 8 percent average annual rate of growth over the past four decades into five proximate causes, using a growth-accounting methodology. The initially huge importance of physical capital formation, which gradually diminished in favor of productivity growth, is discussed. The current account of the balance of payments recorded deficits during the first two decades after independence that were sustainable. National saving has risen unabatedly to extraordinary levels. Rapidly expanding overseas assets during the past two decades should provide Singapore with an additional income stream from abroad, while the domestic economy continues its transformation.

Chapter 2 probes the conditions that Singapore faced in 1965, the year it achieved independence. What were the strengths and obstacles

3 World Bank (1993) and World Bank (2005b), p. 78.

delivered by history and geography? Did Singapore start with a favorable position on balance? Or did it play well the cards it was dealt through astute policies and institutions?

Chapter 3 examines the policies behind the proximate sources of Singapore's economic growth. Four general principles of sound pro-growth economic policy design are identified that apply to other countries as well. This chapter also shows how various policies in Singapore (fiscal, compulsory saving, monetary and exchange rate policy, wage policy, education, health, and road transportation) illustrate the importance of these basic principles. Policies are shown to have addressed binding constraints as they evolved. The heavy hand of the state in the economy is discussed separately, as specific to Singapore.

Chapter 4 explores how good policies were actually implemented in Singapore. Many countries design good policies, sometimes with external help, but fail in their implementation. Policies in Singapore were supported by the right institutions: good governance, the rule of law, and a well-functioning social contract resulting in political stability. These institutions, in turn, benefited from specific values in society, which the government also promoted.

Chapter 5 examines the political economy of creating pro-growth institutions. Why and how did Singapore succeed, where other countries fail, in creating growth-enhancing institutions? One intriguing answer is that the ruling elite found it to be in its own interest to spread the benefits of economic growth widely. What strategic and tactical principles were followed that might be relevant elsewhere?

Chapter 6 pulls the different strands together and addresses prospects and challenges for future growth in Singapore. Deficiencies in democracy vex Western critics, but preserving racial harmony and coping with immigration are of concern to many Singaporeans (George, 2000). We conclude the chapter with lessons that other countries might learn.

I have tried to make the book appealing to a wider audience, while meeting professional standards. Accordingly, technical details have been relegated to footnotes. These notes also provide leads to readers who might find the book a useful template for further work on their own, including comparing growth experiences of other economies with Singapore's. After reading this book, readers may well conclude that Singapore is a very special and unusual place. I hope it will become less enigmatic, having revealed insights of value to other countries.

One The Sources of Economic Growth in Singapore

Background

In 2005, Singapore celebrated its 40th birthday as an independent nation. During these four decades, the population of this small city-state, located at the southern tip of the Malay peninsula, grew to 4.35 million, more than twice the number in 1965. Meanwhile, the economy, as measured by real Gross Domestic Product (GDP), multiplied by over 20 times.[1] What were the factors behind Singapore's remarkable economic success since 1965, and how did it manage to become an advanced economy in just 40 years?

Retrospective economic studies sometimes take 1959 as their starting point. In that year, the British relinquished power over most internal government affairs, having ruled Singapore since 1819 because of its valuable deep water port and strategic location. The PAP won the elections in 1959 and has governed Singapore ever since. Lee Kuan Yew became the country's first prime minister and remained in that position for the next 31 years. Since 1990, he has continued as a senior cabinet member. Key institutions at the heart of Singapore's success, such as the Economic Development Board (EDB) and the Housing and Development Board (HDB) were established as early as 1961, by transforming their rudimentary predecessors from colonial times.

From 1963 to 1965, Singapore was part of the Malaysian Federation. Its government had pressed for accession, mainly for

1 Unless otherwise indicated, data in this chapter on Singapore's population, GDP and its components, labor force, and unemployment originate from the website of the Department of Statistics, Singapore, http://www.singstat.gov.sg.

economic reasons. Political and economic union with Malaya doubled the size of the market in terms of GDP. This larger scale facilitated cost-effective production in Singapore of manufactured items that had until then been imported. Secure access to raw materials was a further motive. So was politics. Malaya and the British saw in the union a way to help Lee, and themselves, prevent Singapore, then a hotbed of communist agitation, from becoming an Asian Cuba. From the outset, however, ethnic tension between the two territories ruled. The Malayan government, under Tunku Abdul Rahman grew increasingly resentful of the PAP's assertiveness in federal politics, viewing it as a Chinese bid to challenge Malay supremacy. The escalating discord led to major racial riots in 1964, which set the stage for Singapore's separation from the Federation a year later and its traumatic birth as a nation.

THE GROWTH RECORD

Singapore experienced exceptionally high economic growth during the 40 years since its independence. GDP at constant prices rose at an average annual rate of 8 percent in 1965–2005. With population growth at 2.1 percent, per capita GDP increased by 5.8 percent on average each year. In 2004, Gross National Income (GNI), which adds to GDP net income earned abroad by individuals and firms located in Singapore, was S$41,819 per inhabitant , equivalent to US$24,741 using the prevailing exchange rate for the Singapore dollar (S$) that year. In comparison, per capita income in the United States was US$39,640 in 2004.[2] The preferred practice, however, when comparing across countries is to use an artificially constructed exchange rate that corrects for the difference in purchasing power

2 International Monetary Fund, *International Financial Statistics*, calculated from the U.S. country page.

between US$1 in the United States and S$1 in Singapore.[3] Using this purchasing power parity (PPP) method, Singapore's per capita income in 2004 was slightly higher at PPP$26,590.[4]

National income *levels*, expressed in PPP dollars, can also be used to compare *rates* of economic growth of different countries. Figure 1.1 compares the economic growth performance of 107 countries in 1960–2000. Only one country, Singapore, registered an average annual economic growth rate of 7–7.5 percent (on an aggregate, not per capita, basis); in comparison, 16 countries grew by 2.5–3 percent, including the United States, France, and India.

Several observations can be made. First, Singapore along with Taiwan, South Korea, and Hong Kong experienced remarkably rapid growth. However, being No. 1 in this figure is unimportant in itself: this is not a "winner takes all" contest, fortunately. Moreover, it is not obvious that a contest should be defined in this way, given the limitations of GDP as an indicator of overall well-being. Further, comparing over a more recent period would move Singapore down the ranking and push up countries such as China and India. However, and this is important, substantial differences between growth rates, sustained over a long period, result in dramatically different income levels due to the power of compounding.

Second, mature economies, such as the United States and Britain, grew more slowly in 1960–2000 as they did not benefit from the

---

3 Market exchange rates can be misleading when used for comparing income levels across countries because they tend to understate the standard of living in poorer countries. The reason is that the cost of living is lower than in rich countries; for example, compare the price of a haircut in New Delhi and in New York using the market exchange rate. The bias can be corrected by using artificially constructed exchange rates that better reflect the local purchasing power of different national currencies.

4 Source: World Bank, (2005a), *World Development Indicators*, Table 1.1. Caution is nonetheless urged with PPP dollar measures. World Bank data listed Singapore in 1999 as the third-richest country in the world, after Switzerland and the United States. Singapore's per capita income in that year exceeded PPP$27,000. The number fell to PPP$24,180 by 2003, pushing Singapore into 30th place. The drop occurred despite 8 percent cumulative real per capita GDP growth in Singapore during those four years and negligible changes in consumer price inflation and the market exchange rate in terms of the U.S. dollar.

Figure 1.1 The Distribution of Growth Rates, 1960–2000

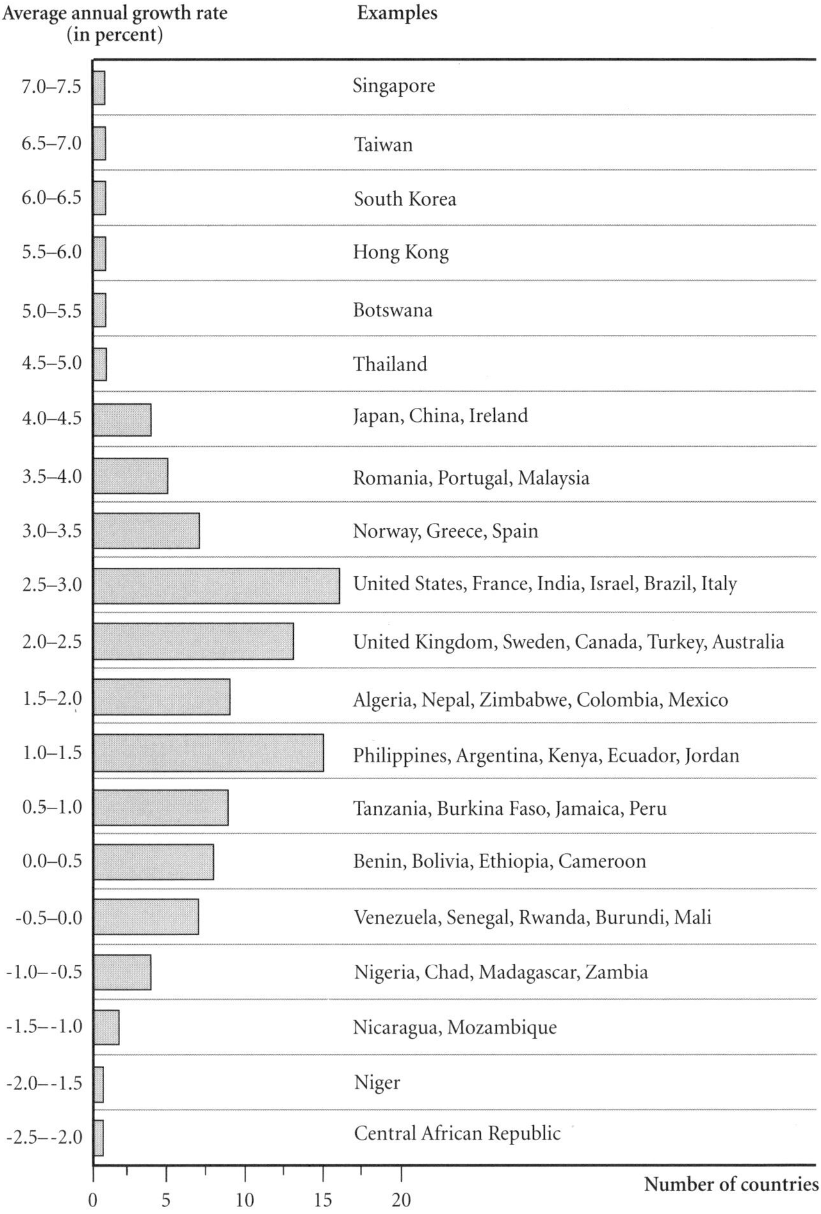

Source: Weil, D. (2005). *Economic Growth*, Figure 1.6, p. 15; based on Heston, Summers, and Aten (2002). ©2005 Pearson Education, Inc. Reprinted with permission.

catch-up effect. Third, Singapore's performance stands in stark contrast to that of the, mainly African, countries who registered negative income growth rates. Given their rapid population expansion, these countries suffered an even steeper absolute decline in their per capita income levels. Fourth, when population growth is included in the picture, Singapore's per capita income converges with that of the United States, rising from under 16 percent of the U.S. level in 1965 to 67 percent by 2004.[5] At the same time, Singapore's success diverged dramatically from the income levels of the poorest countries—for example, Zambia, once a middle-income country, and Nigeria and Venezuela with their impressive oil wealth—illustrating the magnitude of forgone opportunities.

THE QUALITY OF ECONOMIC GROWTH

Output growth in Singapore was consistent over successive decades. The rate of growth fluctuated only narrowly over time. Part of Singapore's success, relative to other countries, stems from avoiding prolonged episodes of slow or negative growth. Economic expansion followed a steadily rising path, interrupted only briefly by recessions in 1985, 1998, and 2001 (see Figure 1.2). After each downturn, output growth bounced back sharply.

Rapid growth was matched by enhanced well-being. The quality of life improved for large numbers of people. Singapore succeeded from the perspective of not only growth, but also social development.

The country pursued economic growth with moderate disparity. Rising prosperity was shared reasonably equally among the population. The Gini-coefficient, a commonly used index that measures income inequality among individuals on a scale from 0 (full equality) to 1 (complete inequality), amounted to 0.42 in the late 1990s.[6] Based on this indicator, Singapore is less egalitarian than the Scandinavian countries or Belgium, where redistributive policies

5 World Bank (2005a).
6 World Bank (2005a), *World Development Indicators*, Table 2.7.

Figure 1.2 Selected Economic Indicators, 1965–2005

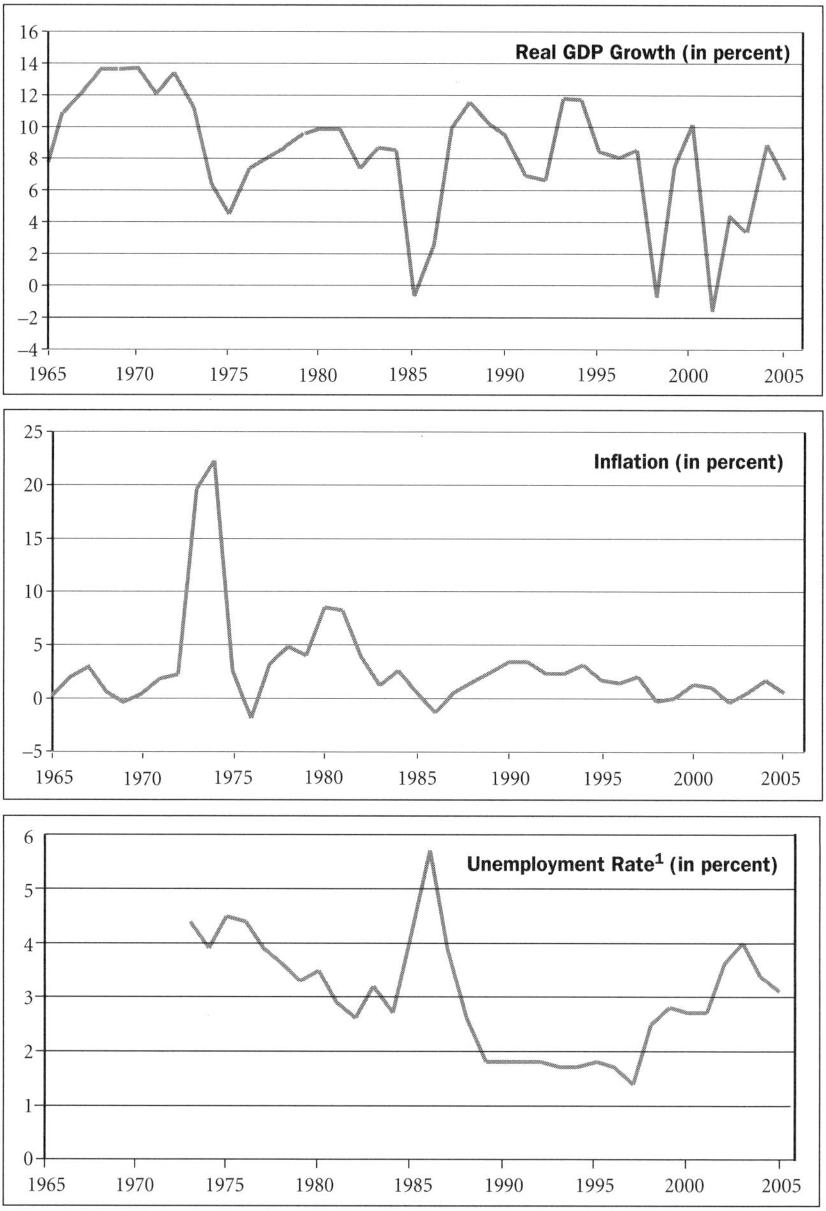

1 Official unemployment data start in 1973. Methodological changes in 1986 (switch from mid-year to annual average) and in 1992 (widening the definition of the labor force) have lowered the reported unemployment rate over time.

Source: Department of Statistics, Singapore (*http://www.singstat.gov.sg/keystats/hist/gdp1.html*) and Singstat Time Series Online (STS).

keep the index at a low 0.25, a level also found in Japan. But income in Singapore is distributed more equally than in Brazil and several other South American countries, where the coefficient is close to 0.60. Moreover, Singapore provided greater equality of opportunity for upward mobility than more stratified societies such as rural India. In addition, assets are widely held: the government's subsidized housing program has resulted in 93 percent home ownership. Even the poorest 20 percent of resident households have, on average, the equivalent of US$80,000 in home equity, a remarkable achievement.[7]

Income inequality in Singapore, measured by the Gini-coefficient, has increased somewhat in recent years. The main reason is income disparity between the various occupations, reflecting the forces of globalization.[8] The upgrading of manufacturing and the development of high-value added services from the 1980s reduced the demand for unskilled workers and increased wage differentials in favor of professional and skilled workers. In professional jobs, earnings are kept high by demand for talent from abroad, while at the other end of the labor market, wages are kept low by a steady inflow of unskilled labor from abroad employed in manual jobs (see the section "Flexible labor market" in chapter 3).[9] This is a challenge the government seeks to meet as it tries to encourage retraining, even for older workers with limited education.

Earnings, including those of the lowest income groups, rose steadily over the past four decades. Workers received real average wage increases year after year, reflecting higher productivity. Strong job creation also resulted in remarkably low unemployment rates, which have averaged 3.0 percent since 1973, and ranged from 5.7 percent in 1986 to under 2 percent for several years during the 1990s (see Figure 1.2).

Poverty levels have dropped steadily and absolute poverty is virtually eliminated. Human development indicators improved markedly.[10] Life expectancy has risen to 78 years in 2003, from 66

7 Prime Minister Lee Hsien Loong, in his 2006 Budget Speech, March 2006.
8 Mukhopadhaya and Rao (2002), p. 101.
9 Peebles and Wilson (2002), p. 263.
10 World Bank (2005a), *World Development Indicators*, Table 2.19.

years in 1965. Infant mortality has fallen from 27 per 1,000 live births in 1965 to less than three in 2003, the lowest in the world along with Japan and Sweden. High standards of hygiene prevail and safe drinking water is available to all.

Growth has been environmentally sustainable. Singapore is remarkably clean and green, despite its population density, earning it the label, "Asia's garden city." Indicators of water pollution through industrial emissions are among the best in the world.[11] But it was not always like this. In the 1960s, food was prepared and sold on crowded streets, with the pervasive heat and humidity resulting in decay and filth; cattle roamed the city center for a brief time; waste of pigs, which at one point totaled 900,000, gave the rivers a putrid stench. Only massive engineering works starting in 1977, expertise, and sustained dedication over many years could produce this remarkable metamorphosis.[12] Singapore has avoided the air pollution of Asian megalopolises like Beijing, except on occasional dry summer days when smog and haze from burning bush in neighboring Sumatra blow in from the southwest, reminding Singaporeans of their vulnerability, and everyone of the world's growing interdependence.

Since independence, Singapore has built an enviable record of religious tolerance and ethnic harmony. Low criminality has resulted in a high level of personal safety. Collective security and social cohesion prevail—there is a feeling of belonging to the nation-state. In 1972, the mainly Buddhist Himalayan kingdom of Bhutan began measuring another indicator in addition to GDP: the "gross national happiness." Its goal is to stress cultural heritage, environmental conservation, and social cohesion. While Singapore is no nirvana—children are apprehensive about less-than-perfect school grades while adults lead fast-paced and demanding lives—economic growth has been accompanied by a high quality of life in many aspects.

Singapore has played a constructive role internationally. As a founding member of the Association of Southeast Asian Nations (ASEAN), it played a key role in helping shape the region, and strives

11 World Bank (2005), *World Development Indicators*, Table 3.6.
12 Lee Kuan Yew (2000), Chapter 13.

for peaceful relations in Asia, aware of their importance, including for the economy. Singapore strongly advocates multilateral trade liberalization but has also concluded several bilateral free trade agreements (FTAs) since 2000, including with the United States, Japan, and Chile, with more under negotiation. While FTAs involve preferential treatment, Singapore views such agreements as a catalyst to speed up trade liberalization within ASEAN.

Decomposing economic growth

What elements have been responsible for Singapore's remarkable performance? To gain insight into this question, a common approach is to decompose growth into the contributions of the primary factors of production, such as physical capital and labor. Labor is typically split into a quantitative component: total number of hours worked in the economy, and the quality of the workforce, which is interpreted as a form of human capital. Human capital is built through improvements in health, but mainly through education and training. Often, however, growth in output cannot be fully explained by growth in all three factor inputs. The residual item—the part of growth not explained by the accumulation of physical and human capital and man-hours worked—reflects higher total factor productivity (TFP), which means increased effectiveness with which the already existing inputs are converted into output. TFP growth comes from technological progress—improved knowledge on how to produce new goods or new ways to produce old goods—and from enhanced efficiency, which is the effectiveness with which factors of production and technology are combined.[13]

13 Weil (2005), p. 504. Note that TFP refers to an analysis that focuses explicitly on at least two factors of production. It differs from the commonly used concept of (labor) productivity, which is defined as output per hour worked—only one factor of production—and therefore captures the contribution of additional physical capital formation under higher (labor) productivity. Equally, TFP differs from the Incremental Capital Output Ratio analysis (ICOR), which is approximated by dividing the investment-to-GDP ratio by the GDP growth rate. A lower ICOR, equivalent to increased productivity of capital, would therefore capture the impact of a growing labor force, which TFP does not.

Whereas technological progress is typically associated with research and development (R&D) or the dissemination of state-of-the-art techniques such as new software, mobile phones, or the Green Revolution in agriculture during the 1970s, efficiency gains can result from a surprisingly wide range of forces in society. These include: organizational improvements, such as shorter turnaround times for ships in port; cost cutting by individual firms by working smarter; legal reforms that reduce uncertainty in capital markets; better incentives for or reduced obstacles to reallocating labor to more productive activities, for example, as a result of more flexible wage determination or the lowering of tariffs on imported capital goods; increased competition that spurs acquisition of new technology; economies of scale; and reduction in privately profitable but socially wasteful activities that redistribute income within society but fail to add to total output, such as civil strife, lobbying, and other "rent-seeking" activities.[14] TFP growth can be negative, at the level of an individual firm when losses are incurred, or at the level of a sector or an entire economy as might result from a prolonged period of drought or when recessions result in substantial overcapacity.

Together, the three sources of factor accumulation and two sources of productivity enhancement allow for comprehensive attribution of an economy's growth. By defining the fifth item—efficiency—as the residual component, any growth in a country's income level must be due to increases in one or more of these five determinants. Further, the various contributions can be added. A country's economic growth record can thus be decomposed, and the contribution of the individual sources of economic growth be aggregated. Using the terminology of the Olympic Games, a pentathlon of five separate events determines an economy's overall score.

14 Weil (2005), p. 283. An economic rent is a payment to a factor of production that is in excess of what is required to elicit the supply of that factor. Extraction of natural resources results in rents, for example, oil produced at under US$10 per barrel and sold at US$60. Rent seeking arises when government policy creates an artificial scarcity such as through licenses or protected monopolies.

ACCOUNTING FOR SINGAPORE'S GROWTH

The results of one application of the above described framework are summarized in Figure 1.3. Singapore's GDP growth in 1960–2003 averaged 7.8 percent annually, compared with 6.7 percent for a sample of seven rapidly growing economies of East and Southeast Asia, and 3.5 percent for a representative group of 21 industrialized countries.[15]

The main findings for the full period of 1960–2003 are as follows:

First, the buildup of the stock of physical capital accounts for more than half of the economic growth that occurred in Singapore over the 43-year period (4 percentage points out of 7.8).[16] Between 1960 and 2003, Singapore's capital stock—which now includes innate objects such as apartment buildings, factories, and machinery—grew at 11.3 percent annually, doubling on average every six years. This is an exceptionally high pace of expansion by any comparative historical standard. This growth rate, multiplied by 0.35 on the premise that

Figure 1.3 Sources of Economic Growth, 1960–2003 (in percent)

	Singapore			East Asia (ex China)	Industrialized countries
	1960–2003	1970–1980	1990–2003		
Total output	**7.8**	**8.6**	**6.2**	**6.7**	**3.5**
Contribution of:					
Physical capital	4.0	4.8	2.6	3.3	1.4
Labor force	2.0	2.8	1.2	1.8	0.8
Education	0.4	0.1	0.8	0.5	0.3
Productivity (TFP)	1.4	0.9	1.6	1.1	1.0

Source: Eggertsson (2004) and author's calculations.

15 This section draws on Eggertsson (2004), pp. 7–8. The Asia sample comprises the economies of Indonesia, Malaysia, the Philippines, Singapore, South Korea, Taiwan, and Thailand. The industrialized countries include Australia, Austria, Belgium, Canada, Denmark, Finland, France, Germany, Greece, Iceland, Italy, Japan, the Netherlands, New Zealand, Norway, Portugal, Spain, Sweden, Switzerland, the United Kingdom, and the United States.

16 Economists distinguish between a "stock," which is measured at a point in time, and a "flow" such as investment, which occurs over a period of time. Stock originally referred to livestock, with the word "capital" being derived from the Latin "caput" as in "head" of cattle, one of the earliest forms of wealth and factor of production.

capital contributes about one-third and labor about two-thirds of total output, produces the abovementioned 4 percentage point estimate (for further discussion of this methodology, see the section "The growing relative importance of TFP").

Second, increased labor input—measured as total hours worked and thus uncorrected for quality improvements—accounted for over a quarter (2 percentage points) of the economic growth in 1960–2003. This is slightly higher than in the East Asian economies and substantially more than in the industrialized countries. Total hours worked rose by 3 percent annually on average, compared with the population growth of about 2 percent. One reason for the increase in hours worked was the absorption of initially high unemployment. Electronics assembly work expanded at companies like National Semiconductor, who arrived in the late 1960s. Their requirement for repetitive manual operations created jobs for Singapore's unskilled, uneducated workers. More importantly, the labor force grew rapidly. In part, this reflected natural population growth as young workforce recruits outnumbered the newly retired. Also, tight labor market conditions encouraged women to join the workforce in large numbers: female labor force participation rose from 28 percent in 1970 to 54 percent in 2004. Immigration and the demand for temporary workers from neighboring countries also added to the employed. The swift expansion of the domestic labor force, supplemented by a rising number of expatriate workers, was nonetheless dwarfed by the much more rapid growth in physical capital. In a marked capital deepening, the capital-labor ratio rose about 28-fold during 1960–2003.

Third, the combined contribution of the remaining three sources amounted to slightly under a quarter of the observed economic growth. Of these, the improvement in human capital, measured as the average years of schooling completed, accounted for 0.4 percentage points of Singapore's economic growth. Significant improvements in the quality of the workforce, measured by educational level, took place, partly in response to the scarcity of labor. Interestingly, this is one source of economic growth for which the other rapidly growing East Asian economies were somewhat ahead of Singapore. Strict merit-based standards governed access to continued education in Singapore, resulting in a slightly slower pace of increase in average years of schooling until 1985 than in some other Asian countries that emphasized widening educational opportunities. Against this, international comparisons of average years of schooling of the population of 15 years and older, might overlook Singapore's high educational standards, as reflected in top international results being achieved for mathematics and sciences.[17] Also, on-the-job training was extensive and many working adults enrolled in evening education programs.

Fourth, TFP growth accounted for less than one-fifth of Singapore's economic growth. Empirical estimation difficulties often make it impossible to identify separately the contributions of technological progress and efficiency gains. The common practice, therefore, is to combine their joint contribution into a single score, labeled "productivity growth." TFP growth in Singapore, measured as the residual item, reflects various influences. Interpretations have stressed the adoption of more advanced production techniques in manufacturing and improvements in the quality of imported capital equipment that embodied sophisticated foreign technologies. Cost reductions that were made possible by increasing returns to scale as MNCs expanded their activity, also played a role. Since micro-economic policy distortions in Singapore were limited to begin with (see Chapter 3), reallocation to more productive sectors of the economy as a result of structural policy reforms offered narrower scope for TFP growth than in distorted economies, such as China after 1978.

In conclusion, the much higher economic growth in Singapore than in industrial countries overwhelmingly results from higher accumulation of physical capital and an increase in total man-hours worked. A similar difference also set the other East Asian countries apart from the industrial ones.

17 Singapore scored the highest among 46 countries in the performance of eighth-grade students for mathematics and sciences. See http://nces.ed.gov/pubs2005/timss03.

THE GROWING RELATIVE IMPORTANCE OF TFP

Economic growth in Singapore and the relative importance of its five sources changed over time. Growth decelerated, from an average rate of 8.6 percent in 1970–80 to a more sustainable 6.2 percent in 1990-2003 (see Figure 1.3).

The forces behind the economic expansion also changed: input growth in the form of physical capital and hours worked explained a much larger share of growth in the earlier decades than in recent years. The steep growth in output in the early years was due largely to the rapid growth of factor inputs in export-oriented foreign MNCs. Massive investment in public housing also contributed. The long-term difficulty, however, with input-driven growth in any economy is that it cannot be sustained indefinitely. Eventually, all "surplus" labor would have been transferred into the more productive modern sectors. There is a limit on the proportion of people aged 15–64 who work. Capital input as a source of economic growth is limited as well: as the capital stock increases, diminishing returns on each additional unit push down the marginal product of capital eventually to zero. In addition, a growing capital stock requires an increasing share of a country's saving just to replace the portion of the stock that has depreciated due to wear and tear or obsolescence.[18]

Since 1990, education and productivity growth have increased their combined contribution to economic growth to nearly 40 percent (2.4 percentage points). The contributions of increases in capital stock and labor input have leveled off, as is expected in a maturing economy. Singapore's economy saw the average capital-output ratio rise from about 1 in the 1960s to more than 3 by 2000. As growth fell to a more sustainable level, input-driven growth was replaced by "quality" growth from gains in education and in TFP as huge earlier investments in infrastructure were bearing fruit.

The 1985–86 recession, the first since 1964, triggered major changes in Singapore's economy that contributed toward this shift to

18 Diminishing returns and depreciation are at the core of the neo-classical growth model developed in 1956 by Robert Solow, 1987 Nobel Prize laureate in economic sciences.

quality-based growth. The recession demonstrated the city-state's vulnerability to demand contraction in the United States and its global ripple effects, as well as to relocation by MNCs from Singapore to lower-cost countries in the region. Other contributing factors included the oversupply in the construction industry due partly to extensive house-building and the failure of the "high-wage policy" (see the section "Pragmatic policy adaptation and correction" in chapter 3). The government reacted to these challenges by steering industry away from the simpler repetitive assembly tasks and toward industrial upgrading with higher value-added. Banking and other service sectors were given greater prominence. Schooling and higher-level engineering became increasingly important. In the 1990s, Singapore decided to transform itself into an innovation-driven and knowledge-based economy. In Singapore, performance in educational attainment and R&D—arguably the two most important determinants of technological capability—had lagged the progress made in Taiwan, Hong Kong, and South Korea. Concerted efforts were taken to catch up in human capital formation and productivity.

An academic debate in the early 1990s further spurred the government to sustain economic growth in Singapore through greater reliance on productivity enhancement and innovation. A large and controversial literature, involving Alwyn Young (1992) and Paul Krugman (1994), came up with growth-accounting results that attributed an even larger share of Singapore's growth to physical capital formation than depicted in Figure 1.3. Young found TFP, which is the residual item and therefore sensitive to errors made elsewhere in the exercise, close to zero. This finding implied that Singapore's economic growth was bound to decelerate sharply because only TFP growth, and not factor inputs, can ensure sustained economic growth in the long run.[19] More than 10 years on, the controversy has abated, and while questions remain, the

19 Much of the early pessimism about TFP growth was calculated by Singapore economists, including Tsao Yuan (1986), using official data. See Peebles and Wilson (1996), pp. 200–9.

methodology underlying the numbers in Figure 1.3 is sufficiently robust to provide valuable insights.[20]

Investment and Saving

The rapid growth of physical capital in Singapore reflects impressive annual additions through high levels of net investment. *Gross* fixed capital formation, which includes depreciation, is however a more commonly followed indicator, in view of substantial uncertainty about the annual rate of wear and tear and obsolescence of the existing capital stock. Further adding changes in inventories gives gross domestic capital formation or investment. Singapore's investment ratio more than doubled, from about 20 percent of GNI in 1965 to over 40 percent in the early 1980s.[21] Massive private sector investments took place in machinery, transportation equipment, construction of manufacturing plants, and big-ticket items such as petrochemical complexes. Public sector investment complemented private investment and enhanced its returns by focusing on public housing construction in the early years and subsequently on infrastructure, including an efficient modern port, an airport, roads, and mass transport and telecommunication systems. The investment

---

20 The controversy arose from a variety of methodological problems: (i) specification of the production function, which need not be constrained to constant returns to scale; (ii) the difficulty in estimating the output elasticity of capital from factor shares given limited data availability and in the presence of imperfect competition; and (iii) problems in measuring the growth of the capital stock based on cumulative net investment data involving different vintages and quality (see Eggertsson (2004), p. 6; World Bank (2005b), p. 47; and Peebles and Wilson (2002), pp. 58–66). If the output elasticity of capital is indeed unusually large in Singapore—to the order of 0.5 as Young and Krugman inferred—compared with 0.35 in a typical economy, then under the simplifying assumptions of this methodology, almost all of Singapore's growth must be attributed to the increase in the physical capital stock, given its very rapid growth. By implication, the contribution of productivity growth, being the residual item, then becomes negligible. The controversy has abated due to reinterpretations of the statistical database for Singapore that better justify the common assumption of an elasticity of about 0.35 as in the exercise that underlies Figure 1.3 (see also Wu and Thia (2002), and Hsieh (2002)).

21 GNI (called GNP in an earlier methodology) is a more comprehensive measure of income than GDP. GNI in Singapore has turned slightly lower than GDP in recent years, as rising payments to expatriate workers in Singapore and profit remittances from Singapore have exceeded inflows earned on Singapore's investments abroad.

ratio continued to exceed 30 percent in the 1990s (see Figure 1.4). It dropped thereafter to below 20 percent in 2003 and 2004 as Singapore's economy suffered the fallout from the September 11, 2001 terrorist attack and the Severe Acute Respiratory Syndrome (SARS) scare in 2003, causing a slump in construction activity and a sharp reduction in inventories.[22] Nonetheless, for 1965–2004, Singapore's investment ratio was exceptionally high compared to other countries, including in East Asia.

Figure 1.4 Saving and Investment Ratios, 1965–2005 (in percent of GNI)

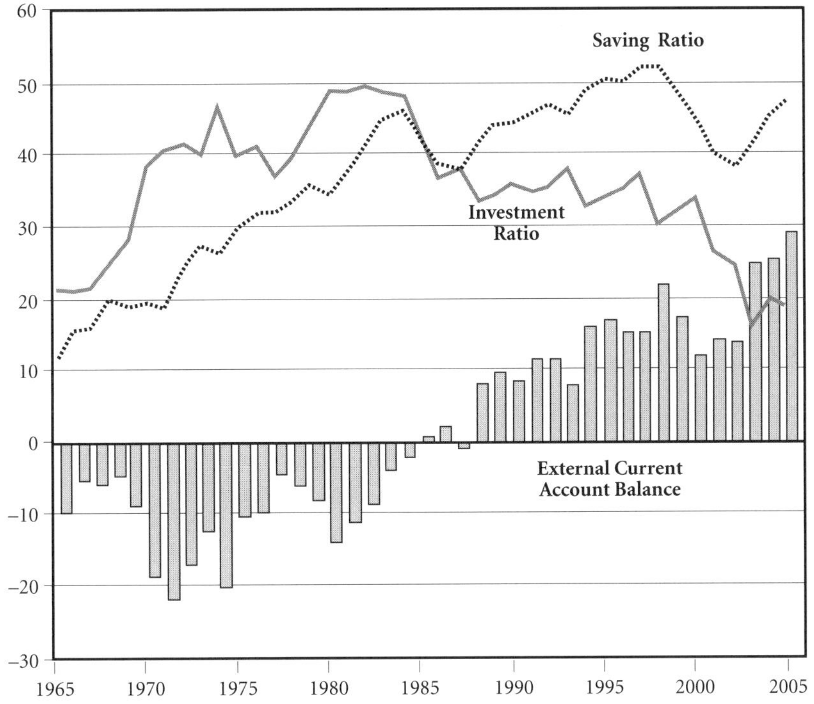

Source: Singapore Department of Statistics, STS (Singstat Time Series Online).

22 Inventories in relation to GNI fell 9 percentage points in 2003 and a further 6 percentage points in 2004, unusually large compared to other economies. This may be related to the fact that "domestic" merchandise exports, which exclude reexports, are also exceptionally large, amounting to 105 percent of GDP in 2005. Reexports of merchandise imported into Singapore but not "processed" locally (although possibly split into lots, graded, and sorted) amounted to 92 percent of GDP, bringing total exports to 197 percent of GDP in 2005.

Singapore's high investment level was facilitated by high saving. The share of GNI that was not consumed rose steadily at times exceeding 50 percent in the 1990s. In several of the 40 years under consideration, Singapore recorded the world's highest saving ratio. Since 2000, the ratio has averaged 43 percent, an order of magnitude that Singapore shares with only China and, at times of high international petroleum prices, with a few oil-exporting countries such as Saudi Arabia.

Until 1985, Singapore's domestic investment exceeded its national saving. The current account of the balance of payments registered the corresponding deficits. Financial capital inflows from abroad supplemented domestic saving to fund domestic investment. Inflows took the form mainly of foreign direct investment (FDI) as MNCs built factories and brought in equipment or engaged in mergers and acquisitions. Loans incurred by the Singapore government in the initial years from multilateral agencies such as the World Bank were soon repaid. For several decades now, Singapore has had no official external debt.

Expanding Singapore's economy abroad

The year 1985 was pivotal. In the aftermath of the recession that year, the government took the strategic decision to encourage Singapore residents—public and private—to invest abroad. As its own economy matured and was running into supply-side constraints, profitable opportunities opened up in capital-scarce countries that would generate an additional diversified source of income. Also, net capital outflows alleviated pressure to appreciate the Singapore dollar. Rapidly growing current account surpluses provided the funding, as exports grew faster than imports. From a net user of savings from abroad, Singapore became a net provider. This occurred in several ways. First, the Singapore government, mainly through its holding companies, in particular Temasek Holdings, and the Government of Singapore Investment Corporation (GIC), invested part of its budget surpluses in foreign ventures. Examples include an information technology park in the Indian city of Bangalore, hotels in Vietnam, and port facilities and telecommunications in Belgium. Second, since the current account surplus was more than sufficient to fund the net capital outflow, the Monetary Authority of Singapore (MAS), the country's central bank built up substantial official foreign exchange reserves year after year. Third, many high-tech firms residing in Singapore expanded into neighboring Malaysia because of lower land and labor costs. They established manufacturing operations there while retaining their headquarters and R&D facilities in Singapore, taking advantage of complementarities.[23] At the same time, FDI flows into Singapore continued strongly as the country succeeded in building up advanced technology and innovation capabilities, supplementing the current account surplus as a source of funds.

With saving exceeding domestic investment since 1985, Singapore residents—public and private, corporate and household—collectively acquired substantial net foreign assets abroad. On average over the past 10 years, the external current account surplus exceeded 18 percent of GNI, rising to as high as 29 percent in 2005 (see Figure 1.4). On a cumulative basis, this reflects relentless accumulation. Granted, Singapore had run up a negative net foreign asset position by 1985, but given the growth of the economy, the surpluses in the past decade are much larger in absolute amounts than the deficits incurred before 1985. Singapore's official foreign reserves amounted to S$184 billion at end-2004, equivalent to 105 percent of that year's GNI. The country's officially reported net international investment position at end-2004 was the equivalent of 85 percent of GDP—surprisingly low in light of the large cumulative current account surpluses built over the years, probably reflecting conservative valuation of assets.[24] Looking ahead, Singapore's growing net foreign

---

23 Peebles and Wilson (2002), p. 188.

24 Finance Minister Richard Hu (1999) confirmed this line of thinking before Parliament. See also IMF, *International Financial Statistics*, November 2005, p. 864. The net amount reported for end-2004 remained unchanged in U.S. dollar terms over the preceding two years, despite large current account surpluses, appreciation of other major currencies against the U.S. dollar, and generally rising international capital markets.

investment position holds prospects for providing a substantial additional income stream.

The country's switch, from 1985 onward, from a net user of savings from abroad to a net provider, raises interesting issues. First, the earlier growth strategy of incurring current account deficits was fully justified: FDI provided a stable source of funding for rapid export-led growth. At no time did the sustainability of the balance of payments come under threat.[25] Second, like some other Asian countries, Singapore's policy stance over the past 20 years could be characterized as "mercantilist," reflecting persistent accumulation of foreign assets through an external current account surplus that reflects very high saving. Such a policy is contingent on other countries' willingness and ability to sustain corresponding external deficits. Singapore has reached the point where the magnitude of its surplus becomes significant in absolute terms from a systemic perspective and might be assessed in the context of an orderly rebalancing of global disequilibria. Third, despite its high external current account surpluses, Singapore still has a negative net income balance. During the 1990s, GNI exceeded GDP, but this differential was reversed from 2000. Since then, profit repatriation and outbound worker remittances have exceeded earnings on Singapore's investments abroad. This reversal reflects a low international interest rate environment, along with growing dependence on expatriate workers and professionals. Continuing current account surpluses and rates of return on Singapore's foreign assets that are more in line with those earned by foreign companies in Singapore will likely reward the country's extraordinary saving efforts with an additional net income flow from abroad in coming years.

25 External current account deficits of 4–6 percent of GDP can be sustainable under the right growth-promoting circumstances and depending on the type and usage of the financial inflows. South Korea is an extreme example of sustainable external borrowing, with net capital inflows averaging 9 percent of GDP during 1953–80.

Exceptionally High Saving

Singapore's exceptionally high saving ratio is intriguing. Econometric studies have emphasized the role of demographic developments in rapidly raising Singapore's saving rate between 1970 and 1983.[26] The proportion of working-age (15–64 years old) population to total population increased steadily, from 56 percent in 1968 to 70 percent in 1983, as the proportion of young and aged dependants declined. The fertility rate fell and women joined the workforce. Rapid employment creation resulted in a sharp increase in the active labor force. With fewer dependent children, families lowered the portion of income consumed, thereby raising the portion saved. This is a powerful hypothesis, based on Modigliani's life-cycle theory of consumption, which has been confirmed for other East Asian economies as well. The implications are profound: for Singapore, a lower saving ratio lies ahead as its population ages rapidly in coming decades. By contrast, other economies where population growth decelerates from previously high levels, such as India and Pakistan, are only now entering their saving-enhancing decades. In Bangladesh, 35 percent of the population is 15 years or younger and will soon join the workforce. With fertility rates falling from 6 to 3 children in one generation, the new workers will have fewer dependants, thus allowing the country to reap the demographic dividend, under the right supporting policies. China, by contrast, has already benefited from such a dividend. Similarly in Singapore, the dependency ratio has stabilized since 1983.

Further rapid changes in the saving ratio after 1983 have been associated quite closely with income growth itself as a second explanatory variable.[27] Just as saving facilitates investment and growth, higher growth in turn tends to raise the saving ratio in middle-income economies. Both the central government and the corporate sector experienced an increase in their saving ratios during high-growth episodes in Singapore as their disposable income

26 Bercuson (1995), Chapter 7.
27 Monetary Authority of Singapore (2004), p. 8.

exceeded spending. Limitations on publicly available data have long made it difficult for scholars to separate public- and private-sector saving. Nonetheless, for the years since 1998, a stylized breakdown of the 45 percent national saving ratio seems to indicate about 18 percentage points of GNI saving by private corporations and roughly 9 percentage points each by the central government, households, and the public corporate sector.[28]

Government policies, which are the subject of Chapter 3, were important as well as a third factor in stimulating saving as part of a comprehensive economic growth strategy. The government itself generated savings in the form of current surpluses in its budget, and raised savings indirectly through the surpluses of government-linked companies (GLCs) and statutory boards, and through the mandatory saving scheme that covers over 80 percent of the population. In addition, policies contributed in many ways to rapid income growth and thus to saving as described. A sound macroeconomic and prudential supervision environment encouraged savers to take a long-term perspective and instilled confidence in financial institutions.[29]

---

28 International Monetary Fund (2005), p. 13 and Monetary Authority of Singapore (2004), p. 8. The breakdown is based in part on internal estimates by MAS economists. The breakdown defines the public corporate sector as comprising the major statutory boards and the non-privatized portion of government-linked companies (GLCs). Privately held equity of GLCs is classified under private corporate sector. Starting in the late 1980s, lower saving occurred at the public-sector level and more was contributed by the private sector as statutory boards and GLCs were wholly or partially privatized, and the composition of both sectors changed.

29 Cultural aspects have sometimes been mentioned as a fourth factor. Closely held family businesses in Singapore reportedly have a preference for relying on retained earnings for investment instead of bank borrowing. Another such interpretation refers to deeply held values from earlier generations. Landes (1999), p. 383 relates the structurally high saving in Japan to atavistic values of the classical peasant "who lives for work, and by work adds to his holding; that is his reason for being."

SUMMARY

- Singapore experienced consistently high growth, interrupted only briefly by relatively few recessions from which the economy rebounded quickly, thanks to skillful crisis management (see Chapter 3 for details).
- Income levels rose steadily, but Singapore also succeeded from a social-development perspective.
- Growth was driven by factor accumulation, in particular rapid buildup of physical capital, as reflected in high investment, mainly by foreign MNCs. This created employment for a growing labor force.
- Concerns arising from neoclassical economics about diminishing returns did not produce the dismal outcome that some had predicted, although growth has decelerated to a more sustainable level (5.2 percent) over the past decade. Additional fixed capital formation continues to contribute to growth. Over time, however, the contribution of human capital formation, technological progress, and efficiency gains has become more important.
- Singapore's saving rose steadily from low to exceptionally high levels reflecting demographic factors, high income growth, and government policies. External current account deficits until 1985 proved compatible with successful economic growth. Financing in the form of FDI for export growth was sustainable, and Singapore did not borrow from abroad for consumption purposes.
- After 1985, high saving enabled the buildup of substantial net foreign assets. This should provide a diversified flow of additional income in future years.

Two Singapore's Initial Circumstances

Countries, at any point in time, are faced with a given geographical, historical, social, and political reality. Their development strategies must therefore start from these initial circumstances. Did the conditions in which Singapore found itself in 1965 facilitate the subsequent impressive economic growth? Or were they impediments instead?

Background

Geographical location as a determinant of a country's development has a long and controversial history. The heat and humidity of the tropics were considered early on to discourage vigorous physical and intellectual labor. The French philosopher, Montesquieu, observed in 1748 that "people are less vigorous in hot climates."[1] After World War II, however, intellectuals in the newly independent, former colonies rejected this line of thinking, perhaps not surprisingly. To them, such pessimistic geographical determinism arose as a convenient rationalization by the former colonial powers for the lack of progress of the indigenous populations during their colonial rule.

Current thinking in development economics does assign some role to geography.[2] In Singapore's case, elements to be considered include its tropical location, proximity to the sea, and a dearth of natural resources.

---

1 Montesquieu (1758), Book XIV, Chapter 2.

2 Sachs (2005) emphasizes the role of geography in Africa's plight, pointing to droughts and malaria, in addition to lack of infrastructure and HIV/AIDS.

Tropical areas face disadvantages. As emphasized by David Landes, people must work more slowly in a warm and humid climate if they are to survive.[3] To keep on functioning, the human body must dissipate the heat produced by muscles; cooling stops when sweat can no longer evaporate. Also, while some crops such as palm oil can thrive, tropical climates were generally deemed to be inhospitable to agriculture: torrential rains often alternate with long dry seasons, eroding top soil; the absence of frost favors disease-carrying insects; and parasites thrive in warm, humid climes, thus spreading infectious diseases of crops and humans. Moreover, infections take longer to heal in tropical climates than in temperate zones. Despite such unfavorable conditions, Singapore has managed to eradicate malaria, by draining swamps and taking other precautions; however diseases such as dengue fever still prevail.

Proximity to the sea, by contrast, has long been recognized as being favorable to development, albeit in a loose way. Adam Smith pointed out that "sea transportation is much cheaper than land transportation, so it should come as no surprise that major cities and civilizations are situated on the coast or along navigable rivers."[4] Lower transport costs stimulate exchange, specialization, and a wider variety of products, thereby allowing markets to develop. Openness facilitates transfer of technology and ideas, resulting in higher value-added and more efficient organization of the economy.

Empirical evidence confirms some positive correlation between a country's income level and its remoteness from the equator (see Figure 2.1). Distance from the equator is a proxy for climate, albeit a crude one since it does not take into account elevation or phenomena such as the Gulf Stream, which benefits Western Europe.[5] Similarly, proximity to the sea appears to have some relationship with average income levels (see Figure 2.2). Within large countries, there is similar evidence; for example, China's coastal areas have developed better than its inland regions. But the relationship is

3 Landes (1999), p. 7.
4 Smith (1776), Book I, Chapter 3.
5 Weil (2005), pp. 432 and 434.

Figure 2.1 Relationship Between Latitude and Income per Capita

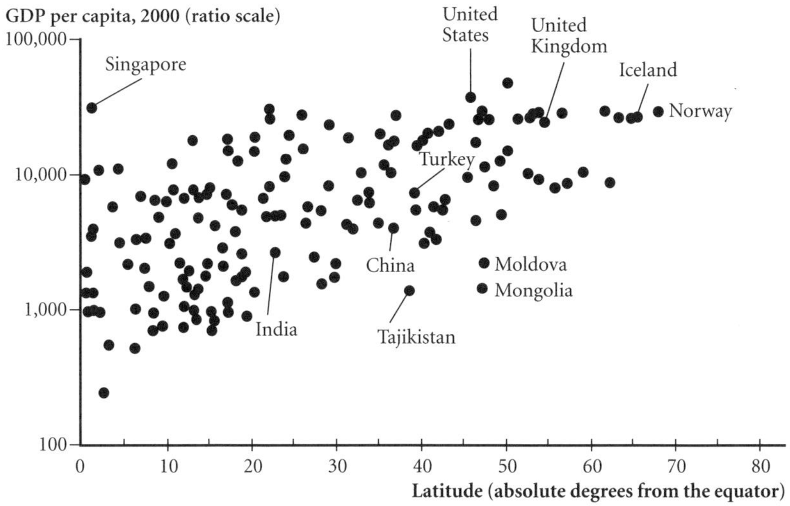

Source: Weil, D. (2005). *Economic Growth*, Figure 15.1, p. 432. ©2005 Pearson Education, Inc. Reprinted with permission.

Figure 2.2 Regional Variation in Income and Access to the Sea

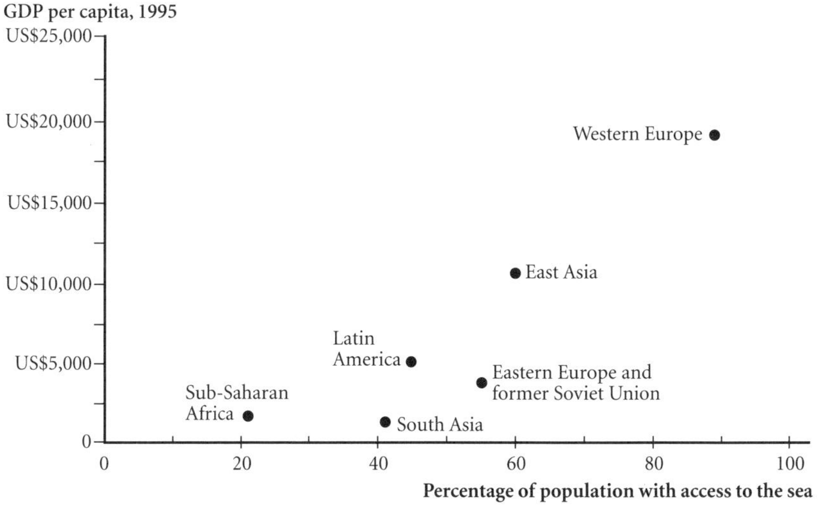

Source: Weil, D. (2005). *Economic Growth*, Figure 15.2, p. 434; based on Heston, Summers, and Aten (2002). ©2005 Pearson Education, Inc. Reprinted with permission.

loose, pointing to the importance of other variables omitted from the analysis. In Figure 2.1, Singapore in particular is an outlier. For once, however, in dealing with economic development issues, causality is unambiguously unidirectional.

How important to development is the availability of *natural resources*? Empirical evidence leads to the conclusion that their presence aids economic growth, but it is neither necessary nor sufficient.[6] There is a positive relationship, but many exceptions make it statistically weak: Japan, has a very high income level but few natural resources, whereas the opposite holds true for Venezuela. Economic growth in the 19th century was driven by the abundant supply of fertile land in countries like Australia, the United States, and Argentina. Against this, however, the availability of natural resources can actually impede economic development. This so-called "natural resource curse" can take several forms. First, the discovery of oil or steep increases in the oil export price have led some countries to borrow—for consumption—against future oil receipts, which in the end did not materialize as expected, leaving these countries burdened with unserviceable public debt. Second, large exports of natural resources can retard industrialization, and the benefits that accompany it, if natural resource exports result in a highly appreciated exchange rate.[7] Third, and probably most important, economic rent from natural resources may have a toxic effect on the political system. It readily invites political corruption, leads to struggle for control of government, diversion of public funds including through lending by state-owned banks to connected parties, which then default (Venezuela), civil war (Sudan, Angola), or foreign invasion (Congo).

A recent study adds valuable insight to this analysis. Rodrik and Subramanian present evidence that geography and history indeed

---

6 This paragraph is based on Weil (2005), pp. 452–55.

7 Sometimes called "Dutch disease," in reference to the setback suffered by the manufacturing sector in the Netherlands in the 1960s following the appreciation of the Dutch guilder in the wake of the discovery and export of large amounts of natural gas.

influence income levels, but indirectly via the quality of institutions.[8] Their study undertakes careful checks to determine the direction of causality among variables that tend to mutually influence each other. They confirm insights emphasized by Daran Acemoglu.[9] In colonial territories where there was plenty of sparsely inhabited land and where the climate resulted in low mortality of Europeans (e.g., the northeastern part of the United States), permanent settlers brought with them European forms of government. By contrast, in colonial territories where the climate caused high mortality rates among Europeans, where there was dense population and natural resources to exploit (e.g., the Caribbean and Latin America), Europeans would engage in the colonial extraction of the economic surplus, and transform—in fact, corrupt—their own institutions to achieve this goal. The institutions created by colonial powers tended to carry over into the post-colonial period, endowing tropical ex-colonies often with bad governments, which in turn stifled economic growth. According to these authors, tropical countries will not experience a negative effect of climate or natural endowments on economic growth, provided they manage to improve their governing institutions (see Figure 2.3).

Figure 2.3 Relationship Between Geography and Income Levels

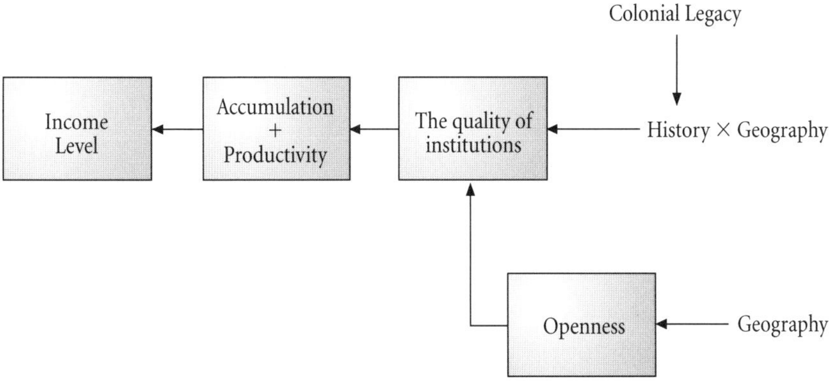

8 Rodrik and Subramanian (2003).
9 Acemoglu et al. (2004).

Economic openness also exerts a favorable influence via the quality of institutions. Singapore's case illustrates their conclusion.

A NEGATIVE INITIAL CONDITION— SINGAPORE'S VULNERABILITY

In Singapore, the adverse prospects for development that faced the young nation at independence are well documented. *Vulnerability*, external and internal, was a grave negative. Independence was caught up in tension with Malaysia and in "Konfrontasi," an intermittent war (1963–66) waged by Indonesian President Sukarno over the formation of Malaysia. Defense expenditure was considered essential, even though there was little budgetary revenue. Singapore depended on the outside world for food, energy, and drinking water. Import price shocks would be acutely felt. The country had no industrial or agricultural raw materials. There was no large domestic market. Indonesia and Malaysia sought ways to export their copra, tin, and other raw materials directly from their own ports, bypassing Singapore as the hub-and-spoke model of traditional entrepôt trade became exposed to economic nationalism.

Internally, there were threats of communism, communalism, and militant unions. The unemployment rate was at least 10 percent and housing shortage was acute. The fledgling state faced the enormous task of trying to create a sense of national identity among a disparate group of immigrants. The population was poorly educated. Industrial unrest was high in the 1950s in the politically charged atmosphere that led to independence. Labor unions—communist and others—were militant and confrontational. They squeezed employers without regard for the financial viability of enterprises. Singapore did not have indigenous industrialists for manufacturing, unlike Hong Kong. Communism threatened. Edged on by China, the Malayan Communist Party (MCP) was fiercely determined to "liberate" Malaysia and Singapore. Racial riots inspired fear. Prospects looked grim for Singapore after its separation from Malaysia, which drew then foreign minister S. Rajaratnam to comment that Singapore had a near-zero chance of survival, politically, economically, or militarily.[10]

Positive initial conditions

From a longer-term perspective, Singapore's *strategic location and natural deep water port* accorded it a crucial development advantage by 1965. Situated between the Indian and Pacific Oceans and on the world's leading East-West trade route, Singapore started out as a processing center of imported rubber, tin, and palm oil from neighboring countries for subsequent reexport. Free trade policies helped develop it into a thriving entrepôt trade center. By the 1950s, ancillary industries such as shipping, insurance, banking, and communications infrastructure had developed. While still quite rural, by 1960, Singapore had evolved far from the fishing village that Raffles had found in 1819. Singapore's merchant tradition nurtured mutually advantageous attitudes, cross-cultural ease in dealing with people from different ethnicity, and an alertness and aptitude to exploit opportunities to benefit from trade and other links with neighbors. The merchant tradition also instilled drive and energetic enterprise, to which a rural agricultural setting, with its seasonal rhythm linked to nature and tendency for social stratification and stagnation, might have been less conducive.

Although claims for independence grew increasingly strong in the 1950s, Singapore had the benefit of a strong *British legacy.* It had been the administrative, commercial, and military hub of the British Empire in Southeast Asia. The legacy included a functioning civil service, political and legal institutions that upheld the rule of law, and the best schools in the region that sent graduates to Cambridge and Oxford universities. The English language remained a unifying factor. Its continuation as the working language facilitated inward

10 In early 2006, Singapore bid farewell to this cofounder of the nation in a solemn and affectionate state funeral. He has been credited with laying the foundations of Singapore's multiculturalism.

investment and would position Singapore well for subsequent globalization. Colonialism had not ended in a bitter and divisive war of independence; neither was it marked by the extractive exploitation of natural resources that resulted in growth-inhibiting institutions elsewhere.

The relatively *recent immigrant status* of most Singaporeans at the time of independence can also be regarded as an advantage. As a young country of second- or third-generation immigrants, even if Malays have rightful claim to earlier arrival, Singapore did not have the internal divisiveness that comes from old injustices. Granted, unskilled labor was exploited in 19th century Singapore, but this did not grow into deep-seated class antagonism. There was no brutal fight for independence as in Vietnam, Indonesia, or Algeria. Without a legacy of past traumas, or subsequent history of nurturing them, Singapore found it easier to forge a collective forward-looking view than, for example the Caribbean countries where Africans were brought in through slavery. The absence of a long common historical experience in Singapore, combined with the dramatic abruptness of independence probably facilitated the reorientation in which the leadership took independent Singapore. The traditional Chinese respect for authority and the mandarin class may also have helped the leadership to steer the newly independent nation in the chosen direction. As a largely Chinese outpost, which had learned the importance of compromising across ethnicity and race, accepting the beneficial impact of incoming MNCs and foreign labor was probably easier than might have been the case elsewhere. Attitudes were probably more malleable and the readiness to change institutions stronger than in more settled societies. Immigrant people, who left their homeland, are more prepared to abandon old habits, less prone to xenophobia being foreigners themselves, and more agile and eager in grasping economic opportunities that will lift them out of the harsh poverty they left behind.

Neutral initial conditions

Some factors have positive and negative aspects. Their net impact on balance is difficult to judge.

High initial per capita income

Singapore had a head start. Its per capita income in 1965 was about 2.5 times that of Malaysia—then, as now, the second-highest in the region—and almost 10 times the levels that prevailed in Indonesia and India, based on market exchange rates.[11] This reflects the city-state's status as a vibrant entrepôt center and administrative and military hub. However, the high-income *level* per se—abstracting from favorable initial institutional conditions—is not an unambiguously positive factor for subsequent growth rates. After a point, the higher the initial income *level*, the more difficult it becomes to sustain a high growth *rate*, other things being equal. As economies mature, they lose the easy growth opportunities that come from copying existing technologies and ways for organizing production more efficiently. In addition, as their capital stock grows, productivity of an additional unit of capital diminishes and a larger percentage of gross saving goes merely to replace existing capital that depreciates, and no longer contributes to output. This explains why Singapore's potential economic growth rate now, when looking ahead to the next 10–15 years is projected to be lower than for countries such as India and Vietnam. At the same time, there is no denying that Singapore's income level in 1965 facilitated saving and investment more than was possible in subsistence economies struggling to survive.

---

11 Singapore's per capita income in 1965 was S$1,567, equivalent to US$512 at the then prevailing exchange rate. In PPP dollars, at market prices of 2000, Singapore's per capita income was about PPP$2,750 in 1965. Note that using PPP exchange rates halves the differential with India and Indonesia from 10 to 5. Based on: Department of Statistics, Singapore website. World Bank, World Development Indicators. *UN Yearbook of National Accounts and Statistics; UN Economic Survey of Asia and the Far East.*

Small size

Singapore's compact size had advantages and disadvantages. On the positive side, the country's small city-size allowed lower unit costs for construction of infrastructure and utilities. Concentration of people facilitated delivery of healthcare and other social services and made it easier to achieve consensus and good governance than might have been possible in a large and diverse country. The amenities of a city made it easier to attract FDI and the foreign employees required to support it. Densely populated areas tend to facilitate exchange and specialization. In Singapore, retrenched workers did not need to relocate to a different part of the country, as public transportation allowed them to take up work elsewhere without the need to change housing. Moreover, once multinational corporations arrived, rapid reduction in unemployment was possible because the scale of their operations allowed them to absorb 10 percent of the labor force by 1973, which was still small in absolute terms compared to larger countries. Furthermore, small-sized countries tend to focus on services since the scarcity of land is a disadvantage to agricultural pursuits.

On the negative side, the small size implied scarcity of land, making housing initially beyond the reach of most. In addition, it has been argued that Singapore's population is suboptimal. Some maintain that Singapore does not have the sufficiently large number of scientists in a specialist field to create the synergies of say, a Silicon Valley. The country's limited human resource base requires it to spread some of its human talent, such as diplomats, more widely. Another factor, the small size of the domestic market, is an old argument that underscored the limitations of import substitution. Following closely was the lack of natural resources within such a small area. Quite importantly, small states are economically vulnerable to global developments and not insulated from exogenous shocks.

Size would not seem to have played a defining role either way. The limitations of a small market can be overcome by open trade.

Many natural resources can be transported across country borders, and size thus proved not to be a negative factor for Singapore. But a small territory is neither necessary nor sufficient for rapid development. China's ascent since 1978 has proved that it is possible, although by no means easy, for a very large country to grow rapidly. Also, other small developing countries have not matched Singapore's performance.

Sovereignty

Is being a city and a sovereign nation an inherent advantage? As a sovereign city-state, Singapore could design its own policies in a flexible manner as circumstances required. To the extent that these policies were designed to serve economic growth well, the ability to chart its own economic and political future was an advantage. As a small sovereign state, Singapore could respond nimbly to new challenges and exercise resilience. Policies could be backed up with legislation. Unlike other cities, Singapore had control of immigration from its hinterland, both in terms of quantity and quality of workers. It could also control access to social benefits of temporary workers. Singapore made income transfers to the surrounding poorer area in the form of workers' remittances but not in terms of transfers through the government budget as might typically be demanded from better-off regions within a country. For this reason, some are of the view that independence for Singapore was a well-disguised blessing. Singapore benefited from separation from Malaysia in some ways, including lower outgoing income transfers and inflow of capital and talent from Malaysia. But Malaysia's growth performance may also not have suffered, despite the loss of incoming transfers. (An intriguing counterfactual speculation, outside the scope of this book, would be whether Malaysia's growth experience would have been weaker or stronger in the event Singapore had stayed within the Federation.)

Achieving sovereign nation status, however, is not a panacea for small states. It has worked for some. Luxemburg is often listed as the country with the world's highest per capita income. It has been able to create a niche, in part owing to financial market specialization that built on regulatory and tax advantages, and as a seat of European institutions. But other small independent island-nations are not development successes. The Caribbean island countries of Dominica and Saint Lucia are similar in size to Singapore but have experienced much lower economic growth and income levels, underscoring the importance to Singapore of favorable factors other than size.

CONCLUSION

Singapore's initial circumstances had negative and positive elements. With the benefit of hindsight, and seeing the impressive successes accomplished over the past four decades, one might conclude that the initial endowments were propitious on balance. But its advantageous location, favorable historical legacy, and recent-immigrant setting did not guarantee subsequent economic achievement.

What is clear is that Singapore seized the chance of becoming a sovereign city-state to exploit to the fullest the innate opportunities offered by its favorable starting point to its own advantage, while at the same time working hard and intelligently to overcome its external and internal vulnerabilities.

Singapore overcame the negatives of its geography and history by switching early on to export-led growth through FDI, building on the strengths of its positives. It engineered an economic strategy whose very success helped overcome the centrifugal forces of communalism. Unemployment, housing shortage, and lack of education in the workforce were all tackled successfully.

Crises spurred Singapore to take new directions, as was the case after the announcement in 1967 of the withdrawal of the British military. Opportunities were created; they did not come out of the blue. An example illustrates this. By the early 1990s, Singapore was ranked fourth in the world, behind New York, London, and Tokyo, in the daily trading volume in foreign exchange. Singapore's initial conditions in 1965 were instrumental in eventually bringing this about. It already had commercial banks, a history of trading in the region, and legal institutions to back up markets—and the geographical advantage of being situated in a favorable time zone. But the government spotted the opportunity of providing international banking services after San Francisco had closed in the evening and before Zurich opened the next morning, making 24-hour global trading possible for the first time. It invited Bank of America in 1968 to set up an Asian Currency Unit to deal in U.S. dollars and other hard currencies. The government also subsequently ensured that all the complementary policies were in place for further development: a stable currency that instilled confidence, building a reputation as a prudent financial center with conservative banking supervisory and regulatory practices, and upholding the rule of law in commercial conflicts.

Singapore had substantial positives but also negatives. These were overcome. Although air-conditioning had already been invented in 1902, only with economic growth did it begin to become affordable in Singapore seven decades later. Beating back the heat and humidity made the city-state livable year-round and raised worker productivity in factories and offices. High saving allowed investment, including enlarging the island: land reclamation added 20 percent to Singapore's land mass in 1960–2005, creating quality space for industrial activities, air and road transportation, housing, and outside recreation.[12] Increased affluence also provided the means to eradicate malaria, in turn improving the health of the population. Singapore turned the small size to its advantage through good policies. The small territory facilitated healthcare delivery compared with large countries with remote areas, but judicious policies were indispensable in helping Singapore be ranked No. 1 in the world for

12 Land area increased from 580 square kilometers in 1990 to 699 square kilometers in 2005. Expectations are for further growth to 733 square kilometers by 2030. Source: http://library.thinkquest.org/C006891/reclamation.html.

the lowest mortality rate of children aged five and below.[13] Labor relations were negative initially with high industrial unrest. As Lee Kuan Yew said: "Until 1962, Singapore had endless strikes. By 1969, there were none. In seven years, industrial relations had been transformed profoundly."[14] Judicious policies and institutions overcame some of the negatives, resulting in virtuous cycles, as will be discussed in the next two chapters.

13 World Health Organization (2006), Annex Table 1.
14 Lee Kuan Yew (2000), p. 103.

Three Pro-growth Economic Policies

Chapter 1 identified five sources that account for Singapore's impressive economic growth from the initial conditions that prevailed in 1965. Over time, the early exceptionally strong contributions of physical capital formation and labor input eased to give way to increased productivity growth and emphasis on education to build human capital. A rising share of total income was diverted to investment abroad, providing an additional earnings stream to complement domestic production.

The next question then concerns the forces behind the proximate causes of growth. If high capital formation enhances a country's growth potential, what in turn propels high capital formation? Specifically, can improved economic policies deliver faster economic growth? How have macroeconomic and structural policies influenced the exceptionally high capital formation and the record high saving that made rapid growth possible? Have policies fostered increased labor force participation and immigration? What role did the government play in encouraging the initially slow but subsequently much larger growth in productivity? This chapter looks at how Singapore's public policies over the past four decades have stimulated factor accumulation and productivity growth in the country.

Fiscal, monetary, and exchange rate policies have ensured macroeconomic stability. Low inflation and a stable value of the Singapore dollar instill confidence among foreign investors and domestic savers while promoting efficient allocation by keeping relative prices transparent. Over the 40-year period, the CPI inflation rate averaged 3 percent, with only one sharp peak, at the time of the

1973–74 oil price shock (see Figure 1.2). Singapore's inflation rate was far below the 25 percent average for the African countries and even higher rates in South American countries during the same period The external value of the Singapore dollar has been more stable in terms of the currencies of the country's major trading partners—including the US dollar, the Yen, and the Euro—than some of these major currencies are relative to each other.

With regard to *structural policies*, Singapore opted for open markets and integration of trade and capital flows with the global economy. Foreign direct investment (FDI) was welcomed at a time when it was rejected elsewhere. Export-led industrialization early on replaced a short unsatisfactory episode of import substitution policies. Meanwhile, government policy encouraged ongoing restructuring into new areas of higher value-added in industry and services, as each decade threw up new competitive challenges. Education and on-the-job training played a key role in building human capital. Public healthcare policies were cost effective, supporting the goal of economic growth. Well-functioning labor markets helped ensure efficient allocation and social stability.

Many countries designed comprehensive macroeconomic stabilization and structural adjustment strategies during the 1980s and 1990s. The aim was to propel their economies onto a higher growth path, often after stumbling into major macroeconomic imbalances that could no longer be financed. Multilateral organizations such as the World Bank and the IMF supported the formulation of such policy programs. While there were many successes, policy programs often fell short of what had been expected.[1] Often, one of the causes was incomplete implementation. But economic strategies were sometimes insufficiently ambitious, failed to focus on binding constraints, or neglected institutions. In retrospect, they were sometimes destined, already at the design stage to deliver disappointing economic growth results.

1 World Bank, (2005b), pp. 7–10.

Singapore's economic growth strategy was homegrown, although the government consulted widely through numerous study panels and advisory commissions to take in lessons from other countries' successes and mistakes. Dr Albert Winsemius, a Dutch economist who led the 1960 United Nations Development Program (UNDP) mission to Singapore, continued to advice on industrialization and economic development for many years thereafter. The IMF held regular consultations with Singapore, as it does with all its 184 member-countries, but Singapore is among a minority of countries that never drew on IMF financial resources.

In this chapter we review economic policies across various areas as Singapore chose to design and implement them. Strong and consistent policies underpinned the remarkable factor accumulation and productivity increases. Instead of describing sequentially the various policies in detail, we distill the salient features of the combined set of policies. The focus is on underlying principles that have wider applicability, and on illustrating how these were applied in Singapore's specific circumstances. Organizing the discussion by key principles of policy design should facilitate comparing Singapore's experience with that of other countries.

THE DISCIPLINE OF BINDING BUDGET CONSTRAINTS

Singapore, as a society, extols discipline as evidenced by orderliness and hard work. All over the world, discipline is admired in sports and the arts for leading to excellence. In the field of economics, however, discipline is unpopular, but not in Singapore. Discipline permeates the government's finances—which have been in overall surplus for all but one year during the past two decades.[2] Discipline is also reflected in high saving- and correspondingly low consumption rates in the

2 As explained below, official government methodology focuses on a variant of the "primary operational balance" and not on the overall balance. Budget deficits were more frequent, if the official methodology is used.

private sector. How have economic policies contributed to high public and private saving? Finally, discipline has also been central to wage policy, which except for some years around 1980, sought to limit wage increases to productivity growth.

Sound fiscal management

Fiscal policy has generated a substantial portion of Singapore's high savings. The resulting resources were channeled into infrastructure, housing, and human capital formation, and in recent decades, into investments abroad. Fiscal policy has thus laid the basis for financial stability, reducing uncertainty among foreign and local investors. It also created complementary public infrastructure, thereby enhancing the profitability of private projects and thus "crowding in" private investment. Tax policy aimed to raise revenue, but was also a major tool for structuring incentives in support of the government's economic growth and social strategy.

Singapore's fiscal conservatism is reflected in high structural surpluses. The overall fiscal balance of the central government has been in surplus every year since 1988. Consolidated accounts that also include the operations of the statutory boards, are not publicly available; this limits but does not invalidate the analysis that follows. A recently conducted study by Jang and Nakabayashi (2005) calculated the surplus at 10.6 percent of GDP on average during 1990–2001. Their study, and the discussion of it in this chapter, follows the methodology of the IMF's Government Finance Statistics (GFS), which focuses on the "overall balance" concept to gauge a country's fiscal outcome. The concept corresponds to the macroeconomic Saving minus Investment balance of the central government. The Singapore government prefers a more narrow indicator of its budgetary position. This officially adopted methodology registers a lower surplus and in fact for some years, a deficit, because the revenue items it excludes (capital revenue and a portion of the investment income earned on government assets) exceed the expenditure items omitted (net lending by the government, interest payment on government debt, and transfers to social endowment funds).[3]

Strict public spending, in particular of current government expenditure, underlies Singapore's strong budget position. Unlike in many developing countries, there is no drain on the budget from loss-making public enterprises or from general subsidies on items such as petroleum products, electricity consumption, or food products. Interest payment on public debt is quite low: the government has no external debt and its domestic debt is limited to government securities issued to provide a benchmark for domestic capital markets and to borrowing by the government from the CPF (see the section "High corporate sector and household saving" in this chapter) for reinvestment or on-lending to other agencies. Singapore also avoided costly banking crises, which in countries such as Indonesia in 1997 and Argentina in 2000 raised the public debt by as much as 55 percent of GDP with an attendant interest burden for years to come.[4]

Unlike in OECD countries, there are no costly welfare schemes: government outlay for social security and welfare amounted to less than 1 percent of GDP on average in 1990–2001, compared with 13 percent of GDP in the typical OECD country. Singapore has no defined-benefit social security program.[5] In Singapore, old-age security is seen as being primarily the responsibility of the individual and the family, followed by the community through charity, with the state acting only as a last resort. There is no formal unemployment insurance scheme: individuals out of work have to rely primarily on accumulated savings or family support. If these are absent, the

3 This astute choice of definition serves the policy purpose of facilitating the generation of large net savings that are added to accumulated government reserves year after year, and the political purpose of allowing the authorities to claim that a portion of the "surplus" thus measured is being "put back in the economy for infrastructure development" or "is shared with lower-income groups in good years for healthcare and education" or that a portion of taxes levied is "returned to the people through transfers of economic growth dividends."

4 World Bank (2005b), p. 102.

5 Public pensions are limited to holders of political positions, the judiciary, and top civil servants and military officers.

government provides a social safety net as a last resort, but this is subject to stringent means-testing. Singapore aims to be a compassionate society, provided the beneficiaries make an effort according to their abilities. Grassroots-based community care programs cater to the needs of those temporarily hit by economic adversity and of the long-term pathetic poor with a view to preventing the development of a self-perpetuating social underclass. In the 2001 recession, the unemployed benefited from rebates on housing rents and utility charges and ad hoc assistance provided on a discretionary basis and in limited amounts.

Concerned, however, about undermining the work ethic, the government resists introducing entitlement programs, emphasizing instead retraining and incentives that foster job creation. Thus, the 2006 budget tops up the wages of older low-income people who are employed at least part of the year as a form of income support to reward their efforts and encourage them to remain self-reliant and not give up working even though they earn little and struggle to survive in an economically advanced society. The financial incentive could be interpreted as a negative income tax, although it is tied to the requirement of holding a job. The one-time bonus is not permanent as the government wishes to study its impact first.

Within current expenditure, Singapore emphasizes outlays for public housing, education, and healthcare. These categories can be interpreted as contributing to investment in human and social capital and are priority areas for the government. But even here, one is struck by the exceptionally low public expenditure in healthcare. Government outlays for healthcare amounted to only 1.2 percent of GDP in 1990–2001, compared with 6.4 percent of GDP in the typical OECD country. Nonetheless, an efficient system has allowed Singapore to deliver quality public healthcare at a substantially lower cost than in advanced economies (see section on Healthcare system), providing high social and political mileage out of public expenditure.

Defense expenditure, to complement diplomacy, is a strategic priority for the government—given perceived vulnerability—and amounts to 5 percent of GDP, quite high by international standards.

Singapore feels it lives in an insecure neighborhood, where there was a history of state-sanctioned violence against the weak. The country's policy is to be prepared to defend itself and be perceived as such. Even military outlays, however, have an economic rationale. The well-equipped modern deterrence force reduces uncertainty. The military undertakes education programs, including higher studies abroad in business administration and public policy for its elite staff, who in many cases subsequently join the government—as did the current prime minister—or start a business career. Also, the mandatory two-year national service for all male citizens and permanent residents aged 18 as the foundation for a citizens' army contributes to developing cohesion across Singapore's different ethnic communities, thus fostering social and political stability.

In all, current government expenditure in Singapore amounted to a low—some would say too low—14 percent of GDP in 1990–2001, compared with 35 percent in the median OECD country (see Figure 3.1). Yet, economies with a low public consumption-to-GDP ratio have been found to be generally also those with relatively high economic growth rates, enabling them to budget for infrastructure and economic development.[6] Public housing has been a major priority for the government. As a result, Singapore has one of the world's highest rates of home ownership, at 93 percent of residents. Land reclamation, the building of Changi Airport, and large public investments in communications and transportation have all added to Singapore's attraction as a destination for private investment.

As indicated in Figure 3.1, the government's total expenditure and net lending (to entities such as the HDB) amounted to 23 percent of GDP in 1990–2001, compared with 37 percent for the median OECD country. Total government revenue, however, was similar, at 33 percent of GDP. Accordingly, whereas the typical OECD country had a deficit of 4 percent of GDP, Singapore registered an overall surplus in its government finances of 11 percent of GDP.

6 Exceptions include Nordic countries such as Finland, where a large public sector has not detracted from international competitiveness.

Figure 3.1 Comparative Central Government Revenue and Expenditure, 1990–2001 (in percent of GDP, period average)

	Singapore	OECD (median)	Korea[1]	Malaysia[1]	Thailand	Philippines
Total revenue	33.5	33.3	18.2	26.1	17.8	17.5
Current revenue	26.5	33.3	17.8	26.0	17.8	17.1
Tax revenue	16.1	30.7	15.7	19.8	15.9	15.3
Tax on income, profits and capital gains	7.3	9.1	5.5	8.9	5.1	5.8
Social security contributions	0.0	8.4	1.3	0.3	0.3	0.0
Domestic taxes on goods and services	4.7	10.6	6.0	5.9	7.5	4.7
Taxes on international trade	0.4	0.2	1.3	3.7	2.6	4.1
Other taxes[2]	3.7	2.5	1.6	1.0	0.4	0.7
Non-tax revenue	10.4	2.7	2.2	6.2	1.9	1.8
Capital revenue	7.1	0.1	0.4	0.1	0.0	0.4
Total expenditure and net lending	23.0	36.9	18.5	25.0	18.3	19.3
Current expenditure	14.0	34.6	13.5	19.7	11.8	16.4
of which: interest payment	1.3	3.5	0.5	4.0	0.8	4.6
Capital expenditure	5.1	2.2	2.8	5.1	6.0	2.6
Net lending	3.9	0.0	2.3	0.3	0.5	0.3
Overall surplus/deficit	10.6	–3.6	–0.3	1.1	–0.5	–1.8

[1] Data for 1990–97.
[2] Includes foreign worker levy, property tax, and estate duty.

Source: Jang and Nakabayashi (2005), p. 17, based on IMF, *Government Finance Statistics*, various issues, and author's calculations.

Tax revenue was only 16 percent of GDP, compared with 31 percent in the median OECD country. The absence of social security taxes in Singapore explains most of the difference. The corporate profit tax is the most important revenue item, even though tax exemptions have been a major tool for attracting foreign investment. Nonetheless, income and profit tax rates have been progressively lowered to the current maximum of 20 percent, as the government increasingly relied on taxing consumption through the Goods and Services Tax (GST), a value-added type tax, and in the process helped businesses stay internationally competitive.

Government revenue other than from taxes has been exceptionally high in Singapore, amounting to 17 percent of GDP, compared with 3 percent in the median OECD country. Such high non-tax revenue is typically found only in countries where the government derives large royalty income from the extraction of petroleum or other natural resources. A few key items account for the difference between Singapore and the OECD countries. First, revenue from the lease of land was substantial during 1990–2001, at about 7 percent of GDP, since the government owns more than 80 percent of the land in Singapore.[7] Second, prudent investment of the large accumulated stock of government assets has provided a substantial income stream to the government, estimated at about 5 percent of GDP annually. This illustrates the power of compounding over many years: whereas the median OECD country pays 3.5 percent of GDP in interest on government debt, Singapore earns an even larger amount on government assets. Third, user fees imposed, mainly for the privilege of owning and using a private automobile, are high in Singapore, as part of the government's strategy to fight road congestion.

---

7 Mukul Asher (2002), p. 403, disputes the notion that the tax burden is relatively low in Singapore. In his view, government revenue from leasing land should not be classified as capital revenue but under tax receipts since its economic impact is similar to an excise tax. The revenue that the government obtains from successful bidders to use (lease) the land for specified periods is spread out over time and is recuperated in the cost of buildings and other land uses. Against this, however, one could argue that part of the corporate profit tax is paid by public sector entities, including GLCs.

On a cumulative basis, fiscal rectitude practiced over several decades and setting aside surpluses during the boom years notwithstanding criticism of stringency have resulted in a substantial net asset position of the government, which was estimated at over 120 percent of GDP in early 2004.[8] This sets Singapore apart from many other countries, where cumulative fiscal deficits have resulted in net public debt, in some cases equivalent to more than 100 percent of GDP.

Fiscal policy can be considered prudent without necessarily requiring cumulative surpluses of the magnitude seen in Singapore. Mature economies sometimes advance the goal of balancing the budget over the business cycle. For less-developed economies that benefit from being capital importers, the recommendation is that the government budget avoid deficits that become unsustainable in their financing. Moreover, the quality and composition of various revenue and expenditure categories are no less important than the bottom line. Nonetheless, the cumulative outcome of its fiscal policy has provided the Singapore government with a cushion to use for expansionary countercyclical policy, as it did in 1998–2002, without calling into question longer-term sustainability or eroding the confidence of financial market participants. This asset position has put the country in a stronger position than countries with large debt and unfunded liabilities. Singapore can confidently cope with looming financial demands to meet the needs of a rapidly aging population in coming years or with contingencies such as a global recession.

High corporate sector and household saving

Depending on the time period chosen, only about a quarter of Singapore's exceptionally high saving can be attributed directly to the outcome of fiscal policy: saving by the central government—defined as the difference between current revenue and current expenditure—

8 Jang and Nakabayashi (2005), p. 16. Comprehensive information on the market value of the government's assets is not publicly available, which could affect the estimate.

amounted to about 12 percent of GDP in 1990–2001.[9] How have government policies influenced the remaining 34 percent of GDP that was saved by households and the private and public corporate sectors?[10]

Economic policies contributed to the high saving performance of households and the corporate sector. The government's policy of running its public enterprises strictly on commercial criteria added to their operational profits and retained earnings, thus contributing to national saving. Monopoly pricing power of statutory boards for utilities and until recently, telecommunications, also contributed. The accounts of the statutory boards are not consolidated with those of the central government.[11]

After-tax profitability in the private corporate sector, (including the privatized portion of GLCs and statutory boards) while subject to cyclical fluctuations, has also generally been high. In part, this reflects a range of government policies aimed at creating a business-supportive environment, including a profit tax rate that has steadily declined to the current 20 percent. This is captured in econometric regressions of total national saving through the importance of GDP as an explanatory variable. It is also consistent with the well-known observation that rapidly growing middle-income economies tend to have high saving rates.[12]

Public policies have encouraged household saving in various ways. First, in the early years, the government's active population control policy—to the extent that it effectively contributed to the

9 If revenue from land leases is reclassified as current revenue, saving by the central government rises and that of the corporate sector declines correspondingly. Distinctions between current and capital expenditure of the government can be arbitrary and may also bias the estimate of central government saving.

10 Internal estimates by MAS economists indicate that the public corporate sector saved about 10 percent of GDP in 1990–2001 (Monetary Authority of Singapore (2004), p. 6). Households saved the equivalent of about 9 percent of GDP, including 2.5 percent of GDP saved in the form of net contributions into CPF accounts (IMF (2005), p. 13). Saving—defined as depreciation and retained earnings—of the private corporate sector amounted to about 16 percent of GDP on average during this period.

11 Asher (2002), p. 418.

12 Monetary Authority of Singapore (2004), p. 8; see also Lim Chong Yah (2004), p. 373, on the S-curve hypothesis for classifying different countries.

demographic transformation—combined with policies that encouraged women to join the labor force, fostered saving. Second, the income tax regime favored saving by gradually eliminating income tax on capital gains and on interest and dividends. Contributions and withdrawals from the CPF are free of income tax.[13] Third, the limited social safety net provisions provided by the government in the event of unemployment or illness encourage individual Singaporeans to rely on their own precautionary savings.

A large portion of household saving takes place through mandatory contributions to the Central Provident Fund. The CPF was started under the British colonial government as a compulsory savings scheme for employees: 5 percent of wages received was matched by a 5 percent contribution by the employer, to provide a modest retirement income from age 55 onward. The CPF is a fully funded defined contribution scheme where accumulated contributions are maintained in a central fund with separate accounts for individual participants. It covers over 90 percent of the resident population. From 1968 onward, the Singapore government expanded the scheme by raising the combined contribution rates from 10 percent originally to a peak of 50 percent during 1984–85, before lowering them again. Over the years, the CPF has been broadened as a saving vehicle by allowing workers to withdraw their accumulated CPF savings prior to retirement, either to invest as downpayment for home acquisition or in approved financial instruments, as well as for consumption of selected health or educational services. In the 12 years to 2004, three-fourths of the people who opted for handling their own investments earned less than the 2.5 percent rate that the CPF pays as a minimum on members' balances; the unimpressive returns were due to the high costs of managing the private funds and wrong timing. Some experts believe that the CPF has imperiled its original function by assuming new responsibilities. The CPF scheme has contributed to household

13 For an overview of the CPF, see Cardarelli (2000), Asher (2004), and the CPF website: http://mycpf.cpf.gov.sg/CPF/About_us.htm.

saving on a net basis, although less now than in earlier decades due to accelerated withdrawals. CPF saving and voluntary saving by households at their own discretion substitute each other to a degree: in the absence of mandatory saving, voluntary saving by households would have been higher.[14] Equally, there is evidence that the very high saving by the central government through budgetary surpluses has, to some extent, lowered household saving from what it might have been otherwise.[15]

To recapture, the very high saving rate in Singapore—and correspondingly low share of private consumption in total GNI—is partly determined by exogenous factors, such as demographic evolution and possibly fundamental values of thrift and preference for financing business expansion out of retained earnings. Public policies, however, have also contributed in several ways. First, they have contributed directly through the budgetary policy of the central government. Second, the government's overall economic strategy fostered high growth, which in turn stimulated saving by the corporate sector, both private and public. Third, household saving was encouraged by the government's insistence on self-reliance of individuals and families, income tax provisions, and the CPF and Post Office Savings Bank (POSB) systems. Fourth, government policies resulted in macro-financial stability and confidence in the banking sector. Large savings created room for high levels of investment, domestically and more recently abroad.

Strong underpinning of monetary and exchange rate policy

Disciplined fiscal policy and high savings provided a solid basis for prudent monetary and exchange rate policies. Discipline also prevailed in labor relations as the government sought to contain wage increases, in line with productivity growth. In 1972, the

14 Bercuson (1995), p. 47, and Monetary Authority of Singapore (2004), p. 9.

15 For evidence in Singapore of partial Ricardian equivalence as this tradeoff is known in the literature, see Bercuson (1995), p. 47 and Peebles (2002), p. 384.

government established the National Wages Council (NWC) as a tripartite body that set annual wage guidelines which, although non-mandatory, were closely followed throughout Singapore, despite full employment.[16] Together, wage restraint and high savings precluded domestic sources of inflation. Few central banks anywhere could build their monetary and exchange rate policy on such a solid foundation as the MAS.

Figure 3.2 Nominal and Real Effective Exchange Rates,[1] 1976–2005 (2000 = 100)

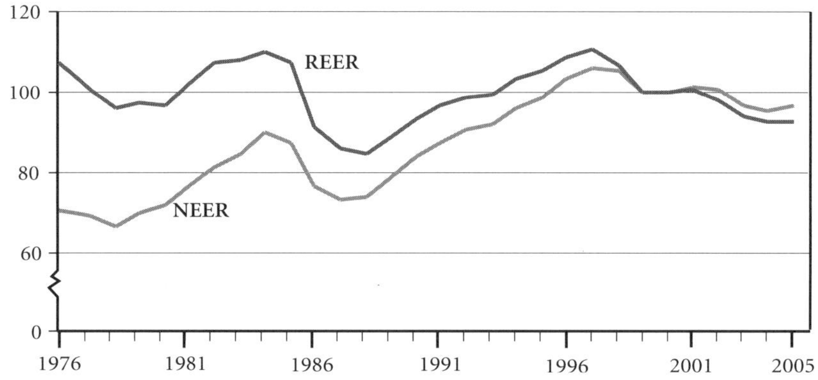

1 The nominal "effective" exchange rate (NEER) of the Singapore dollar is a weighted average of bilateral exchange rates, with the weights reflecting the importance of each partner country in Singapore's trade and as a competitor of Singapore in third markets. The "real" effective exchange rate (REER) is the NEER adjusted for inflation in Singapore relative to that in partner countries. A *lower* price increase in Singapore than in partner countries causes the REER of the Singapore dollar to *depreciate*, for any given NEER. The rationale is that a "basket of Singapore goods," if sold abroad, can then buy fewer foreign goods and has thus *decreased* in value.

Source: International Monetary Fund, *International Financial Statistics*, various issues.

From 1981, Singapore followed an exchange rate-centered monetary policy. Control over domestic sources of inflation freed the exchange rate to neutralize inflation that entered the country via higher import prices. Allowing the Singapore dollar to appreciate over time in nominal terms to neutralize imported inflation helped achieve a low and stable price level in Singapore.[17] Domestic price stability in turn underpinned the value of the Singapore dollar and

16 Lim Chong Yah (1998), pp. 203–4.
17 Monetary Authority of Singapore (2003).

was the main objective of monetary policy. As mentioned, average inflation of 3 percent in 1964–2004 was low by international standards of that period and was considered a remarkable achievement for a country with full employment.

Firm macroeconomic management laid the foundation for rapid export growth. Low and stable domestic inflation facilitated maintaining long-run external competitiveness. The sound value of Singapore's currency has resulted in low macroeconomic country risk. The Singapore dollar was remarkably stable in real effective terms in the long run, while fluctuating over time with changing business conditions (see Figure 3.2). Unrestricted profit repatriation was allowed, well before it became the norm elsewhere. Official foreign exchange reserves, at about US$130 billion in mid-2006 are the highest in the world on a per capita basis. Foreign capital has continued to invest in Singapore, using it as a platform to export to the region and the world. By any analysis, Singapore has fashioned a stable macroeconomic framework. This stability was highly positive for encouraging investment and economic growth and has also helped Singapore weather the 1997 Asian financial crisis well.

MARKET-BASED EFFICIENCY AND ATTENTION TO INCENTIVES

> "*Every individual…generally intends only his own gain…and he is in this led by an invisible hand to promote an end, which was no part of his intention. Nor is it always the worse for the society that it was no part of it. By pursuing his own interest he frequently promotes that of society more effectually than when he really intends to promote it.*"
>
> Adam Smith[18]

Dr Goh Keng Swee, Singapore's first Finance Minister and principal architect of its economic strategy, was reportedly an avid follower of Smith's basic insight.[19] More than other countries, Singapore relies on market-based price signals to set incentives for the behavior of

18 Smith (1776), Book IV, Chapter 2, paragraph 9.
19 Austin (2004).

consumers and producers. Economic policies in Singapore promoted microeconomic efficiency. Distortions were minimized by aligning private incentives with social benefits and costs. For the past four decades, labor and capital markets were flexible, responding to supply and demand. Also, along with Hong Kong, Singapore has long been considered the world's most open economy, highly integrated in global markets. Economic growth is served not only by efficient and effective mobilization, but also management, of resources.

The government followed fundamentally sound market-oriented policies. This does not mean laissez-faire policies. The government subsidizes basic healthcare, education, and home ownership, because of favorable externalities. Further, the government does not refrain from a strong presence of the public sector as producer of goods and services in the economy, through statutory boards and government-linked companies. There is, however, a key awareness of the need to run public enterprises on commercial and market-based principles. Economic rents from lucrative monopolies and concessions, as were granted to relatives and associates elsewhere, are avoided and opportunities for rent-seeking minimized. Public policies were built pragmatically around the legitimacy of using price incentives and market realities as a tool for allocating resources efficiently and avoid waste. Several areas serve as illustration.

Road transportation

Pricing of car ownership and road-use is a prime example. As a small island densely populated with individuals enjoying rapidly rising disposable incomes, Singapore ran the risk of numerous cars choking up the roads. Instead, traffic during rush hour is remarkably smooth, unlike the ubiquitous congestion found in metropolises elsewhere in the region. In addition, air pollution by road traffic is much lower than in Asia's mega-cities. Many countries cope with congestion through land use and public transportation management. Charging motorists for the use of congested roads is less common. In Singapore, the price mechanism and market forces play a key role in meeting people's legitimate transportation needs in an efficient and urbane manner.[20]

Various government charges make private ownership of an automobile among the most expensive in the world. At one point in the late 1990s, an import duty of 45 percent, registration fees, a road tax, and a Certificate of Entitlement (COE) raised the price of a new passenger car to as high as five times its international market value. This multiple has come down sharply since 2003 as the Land Transport Authority raised the supply of COEs it issued and moved instead to restrain actual usage of cars rather than ownership. Since 1990, the government has regulated the growth of the national vehicle fleet in line with the expansion of the road network by auctioning each month a limited number of COEs. Prospective motor vehicle buyers must bid for a COE before they are allowed to make their purchase and each COE is valid for 10 years. The price of the certificate varies with supply and demand. Despite the high cost, car ownership is fairly widespread, in part because of the social status it confers.[21]

In addition, Singaporeans pay heavily for the use of public roadways with private cars. Petroleum products are subject to excise and import duties and are substantially more expensive than in neighboring Malaysia and Indonesia. There is an annual road tax that varies according to engine capacity. To further optimize road use, in light of the high car density, Singapore introduced Electronic Road Pricing (ERP) in 1999, combining regulation, advanced technology, and the price mechanism. On weekdays, overhead gantries strategically located in the city center and expressways scan and automatically deduct a toll from the cash card of a unit installed in each car while traffic moves on. Charges vary according to time, place and class of vehicle. The ERP system allows the optimal use of the road network by making those who contribute more to congestion bear a larger share of the cost of using it.

---

20 Tay (1996), p. 318.
21 Eleven private cars per 100 residents. Source: Land Transport Authority (2004).

Revenue from vehicle-related taxes and charges amounts to over 10 percent of the government's current budgetary receipts, close to 3 percent of GDP. The proceeds help fund large public-sector investments in an excellent public transportation system. Train and bus companies must, however, recover their current costs without government subsidy. In addition, taxi service is widespread and relatively inexpensive compared with other global cities, although again with differential pricing depending on the time of the day and whether a passenger is willing to pay extra to reduce waiting time.[22] An elaborate high-tech calling and global positioning system adds to the efficiency of taxi services.

It has been argued that Singapore's initial conditions facilitated the introduction of price-based road-use policies. Singapore could control the number of cars imported into the country, which non-sovereign cities typically cannot. Its earlier decision to discontinue domestic car production removed one source of opposition to the high fiscal burden on cars. A single layer of government for the whole country eliminated conflict of interest between local, state, and federal governments: people could not so easily vote with their feet and leave the local jurisdiction, since that would mean emigration.[23]

Singaporeans pay a high price for the convenience and comfort of private cars, but most agree with the prime minister that while painful, the alternative is traffic gridlock. Singapore's bold and innovative policies allow the market to allocate resources efficiently.[24]

---

22 Taxi fares in Singapore in 2003 were one-third of those in New York and less than one-quarter of those in London. See Land Transport Authority, Singapore (2004). Analyzing these differences is beyond the scope of this book, but differences in labor costs and overall efficiency are probably significant factors. Taxi drivers may earn the equivalent of about US$40 during a single shift (10–12 hours).

23 Tay (1996).

24 Tan Ling Hui (2003) however, points out that the actual implementation of the vehicle quota system has resulted in some unintended distortions. The number of COEs offered is specified for different subcategories of vehicles. The information needed for optimal sub-categorization under the prevailing system is demanding, and buyers of small, inexpensive cars have paid disproportionately compared with luxury-car owners.

Healthcare system

The Singapore government spent only 1.3 percent of GDP on healthcare in 2002, whereas the combined public and private expenditure on healthcare amounted to a low 4.3 percent of GDP. By contrast, the United States spent 14.6 percent of its GDP on healthcare that year, up from 7 percent in 1970. Spending an increasing portion of income on healthcare as a society grows more affluent makes sense if value for money is received and the financing mechanisms are sustainable. Yet, indicators such as infant mortality rates or years of average healthy life expectancy are slightly more favorable in Singapore than in the United States (see Figure 3.3A).[25] It is true that such indicators are also related to the overall living environment and not only to healthcare spending. Nonetheless, international experts rank Singapore's healthcare system among the most successful in the world in terms of cost-effectiveness and community health results. The price mechanism and keen attention to incentives facing individuals are relied upon to discourage excessive consumption and to keep waste and costs in check by requiring co-payment by users.

Singapore devised a healthcare system that differs from those in the United States and Western Europe. The goal is to provide quality healthcare for all at a minimal cost to society by relying on a combination of public and private service delivery, but without a national health insurance system (see Figure 3.3B). The state plays a key role. Preventing diseases such as HIV/AIDS, malaria, and tobacco-related illnesses by ensuring good health conditions takes a high priority. State hospitals and polyclinics deliver basic healthcare services from the government budget, subject to tight expenditure control. Major use of Information and Communication Technology

25 World Health Organization (2006), Appendix tables. The WHO has developed HALE (health-adjusted life expectancy) indicators as a summary measure of a country's health situation. Note that the United States has a slightly older population and therefore greater medical needs than Singapore, as well as better indicators for morbidity from certain illnesses such as tuberculosis. Against this, Singapore's tropical location is a worse environment for combating infectious diseases.

Figure 3.3A Life Expectancy and Health Expenditure, 2003

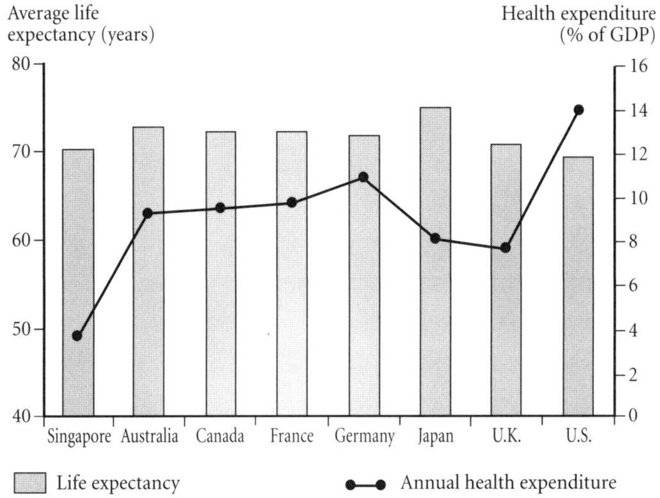

Source: World Health Organization (2006), annex tables.

Figure 3.3B Funding of Healthcare Expenditure, 2003

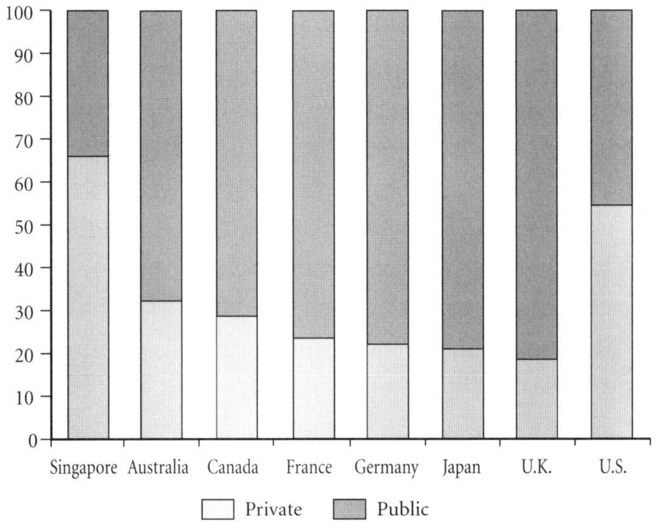

Source: World Health Organization (2006), annex tables.

(ICT) adds to efficiency by giving doctors and hospitals instant access to patients' medical files, and allowing a lower number of clerical staff. An elaborate system screens the use of expensive modern diagnostic tools at public expense to cases where it is fully justified—deliberately limiting choices available to patients and doctors. With health a key public good and important for social equity, basic public healthcare services are 80 percent subsidized through the state budget. The government provides an optional low-cost medical insurance scheme (MediShield) that is intended to support people with long-term or catastrophic illnesses. The insurance covers low-probability, high-cost occurrences—rather than high-probability, low-cost occurrences—to keep premiums down. The state provides a medical social safety net (Medifund) for the truly needy, subject to stringent means-testing, so that no one is deprived of requisite medical care.

Personal and immediate-family responsibility for medical expenses is a fundamental principle. The financial burden of paying for healthcare is placed as closely as possible to the beneficiary, with a view to preventing the high burden on the government budget that typically results from generalized health insurance systems, which tend to be abused. In Lee Kuan Yew's words, mindful of the public consequences of private acts: "We did not want a mentality whereby, after paying a health insurance premium, you consume as much in medical procedures and investigations as you or your doctor can think of."[26] The state recovers 20–100 percent of its public healthcare outlay through user fees. A patient in a government hospital who chooses the open ward is subsidized by the government at 80 percent. Better-off patients choose more comfortable wards with lower or no government subsidy, in a self-administered means-test. There is no common pool of money to "entitle" everyone to the same level of comfort in hospitals. Individuals pre-save for medical expenses through mandatory deductions from their paychecks and employer

26 Lee Kuan Yew (2000), p. 127.

contributions in their individual special Medisave account with the CPF.[27] Only approved categories of medical treatment can be paid for by deducting one's Medisave account, for oneself, grandparents, parents, spouse or children: consultations with private practitioners for minor ailments must be paid from out-of-pocket cash income to discourage supply-driven overconsumption.

The private healthcare system competes with the public healthcare, which helps contain prices in both directions. Private medical insurance is also available. The state mandates publication of private hospital tariffs for comparison shopping. The number of healthcare providers is regulated through admissions to the only medical school in the country and via immigration. Insurance to protect against malpractice litigation, while existing, is not a cost-push factor in Singapore since society is not litigious and there is no trial by jury. To provide a medical safety net, private medical charities form an additional buffer between the individual household and the state as the ultimate resort.

The efficient organization of healthcare, while of value in its own right, also contributes to human capital formation and economic growth by preventing premature exit from the labor force. Cost-effectiveness frees resources for productive investment. Total healthcare expenditures in Singapore have risen, however, from 4.1 percent of GDP in 1999 to 4.5 percent in 2003, reflecting population aging and increased affluence, but less than in the United States where the ratio went up from 13.1 percent to 15.2 percent of GDP during this same period.

27 CPF contribution rates change frequently and vary according to age and type of participant. The total CPF contribution as of January 1, 2006 is 33 percent of wages (up to a monthly wage of S$4,500) for private sector workers under 36 years of age (comprising 13 percent employer contribution and 20 percent employee contribution). Of the 33 percent, 6 percentage points are credited to the employee's Medisave account. Source: Central Provident Fund http://www.mycpf.gov.sg/Members/gen_info/Con_Rates/ContriRa.htm.

Openness of the economy

Singapore's economy is exceptionally *open to international trade*—and thus exposed to global competition and price signals. For many years, merchandise exports and imports combined have been about three times the size of the country's GDP, reflecting substantial re-export, in line with the tradition of entrepôt trade.[28] Access to foreign exchange has been unrestricted and import protection very low for several decades. Import duties presently are levied only on selected items, such as automobiles or demerit goods such as alcohol, and do not advantage the local production. Non-tariff barriers are minimal or non-existent. A short unsatisfying experience with import-substitution policies ended in 1965 with the loss of guaranteed free access to the Malaysian market. The limitations of a small domestic market, dearth of natural resources, and absence of a large pool of indigenous industrial entrepreneurs led the government to opt for integration into the world economy by attracting export-oriented FDI. Competing in world markets required that MNCs were given unrestricted access to imported intermediate and capital goods at unencumbered international prices. Import tariffs on items such as electrical appliances were eliminated by 1975, thus exposing producers to the rigors of international competition. Local producers were thus forced to raise productivity or close down—as happened with the automobile assembly industry. Initially abundant locally available low-cost labor provided the standard Ricardian comparative advantage. A more important contribution of openness, however, was that production for the world market gave the MNCs incentives to bring to Singapore innovative organizational techniques and the best available technology embedded in imported capital goods.

Trade of services is very high and open as well, with international tourism, logistics, and "offshore" financial services being highly

28 According to the Department of Statistics, Singapore, total merchandise trade rose to 369 percent of GDP in 2005.

developed. Nine million visitors came to Singapore in 2005. Nonetheless, protection of selected services against foreign competition has endured longer than in the case of merchandise trade, giving local companies time to build indigenous talent and overcome the limitations of a small home base to achieve critical mass. There was no unfettered free market orthodoxy. Onshore banks (i.e., serving the domestic market) have received protection against foreign competition—partly to allow them to build capital for prudential reasons. The government moved only slowly to broaden the rights of foreign banks to offer various services, such as automated teller machines (ATMs). Only in the 1990s was the infant-industry argument of temporary protection deemed to have become too costly for the Singapore economy, and protection was reduced. Even now the domestic financial sector faces some challenges to fully open up and stay competitive. Singapore law firms are protected: foreign lawyers working in Singapore with a foreign law firm cannot practice Singapore law.

Singapore's economy is highly *open to international capital flows*. It is hard to overstate the importance of foreign resources in Singapore's development. FDI accounted for close to 30 percent of Singapore's gross fixed capital formation during 1985–89. By the late 1990s, foreign-controlled companies produced 42 percent of GDP and over three-fourths of value-added in manufacturing.[29] The liberal climate of welcoming FDI in selected export-oriented sectors has served the country well. As MNCs produced for the export market, they were forced to stay internationally competitive and therefore had an incentive to bring in the best available technology. This contrasts with Brazil and Argentina where foreign MNCs were offered access to a protected domestic market.[30] With regard to short-term portfolio flows, the level of interest rates on Singapore dollar-denominated instruments has been in line with international interest

29 Peebles and Wilson (2002), pp. 14, 69, and 170.

30 World Bank (1993) notes that China also steered incoming FDI toward production for the export market.

rates, but is generally slightly lower to reflect an expected tendency for the Singapore dollar to appreciate over time. Because the MAS manages the level of the exchange rate—by allowing the rate to float freely in response to demand and supply only within a limited range—arbitrage flows under near-perfect textbook type capital mobility imply that MAS has given up control over the level of the domestic interest rate, and that the broad money supply is determined by market demand.[31]

Like other countries, Singapore controls the inflow of foreign labor. Here, too, economic growth has benefited from openness. Augmenting the domestic labor supply is an integral part of the country's overall development strategy.

Foreign manpower made a key contribution to Singapore's economic growth. By 1970, full employment had been achieved and Singapore began to attract *temporary foreign* workers, then accounting for 3.2 percent of the labor force. Their number grew rapidly, reaching 7.4 percent of the workforce by 1980. By 2000, foreign workers made up an estimated 29 percent of Singapore's labor force—5 percent higher-skilled or professionals on an "employment pass" and 24 percent lower-skilled holders of a "work permit."[32] Expatriates filled half of the 600,000 new jobs that were created during the 1990s, with the other half filled by the domestic labor force. The upward trend has continued since.

Foreign workers now play a key role in Singapore's economy. Low-income earners, mainly from the Philippines and Indonesia assist in households and with elderly care, while road and construction workers hail from all over South and East Asia. Professionals and highly skilled workers are being courted through an aggressive open-door policy to attract global talent. Foreigners on temporary work permits and employment passes are expected to leave at the expiry of their term, unless renewed. There are

---

31 The "impossible trilemma" holds that any country that has chosen to be fully open to international capital arbitrage flows can set either the nominal exchange rate of its currency or the domestic interest rate level, but not both.

32 Hui Weng Tat (2002), pp. 29 and 33.

procedures to keep the lower skilled as a revolving pool on fixed employment terms to prevent them from establishing roots. Jail penalties await landlords and employers who house or employ illegal immigrants. Foreign labor and the Singaporean economy have become intertwined in mutual dependence.

In this area as well, Singapore relies on the price mechanism as a policy instrument to manage the total inflow and skill level of expatriate labor. Under the foreign work permit system, employers pay a levy to the government budget that differs according to the skill level of workers and sector of activity. Permits are renewable every two years. Levies are raised if demand from employers is strong. Levies are lower or nil for better-skilled workers. This differentiation has encouraged construction firms to invest in training their workers and to introduce labor-saving techniques. One consequence of improved skill levels is increased competition: during the downturn in 1998, some local employees were retrenched while stronger performing foreigners kept their jobs, unlike in 1985. Also, the inflow of one important category of less-skilled workers may have indirectly contributed to higher productivity. The increase in female labor force participation from 29 percent in 1970 to 53 percent in 1999 has provided more than 228,000 additional workers over the past three decades.[33] This includes 130,000 maids, allowing many families to have a second income-earner.[34] The government explains the beneficial impact of the foreign presence, even though such a policy has led to some concerns among Singaporeans about future job prospects and more intense competition for housing.

Flexible labor market

Labor market and wage policy has been a cornerstone of Singapore's development strategy. Wage policy was adapted over time: the initial

33 The female labor force participation rose to 57 percent in 2005. Source: Department of Statistics, available at http://www.Singstat.gov.sg/keystats/annual/indicators.html.
34 Hui Weng Tat (2002).

emphasis on wage restraint in order to absorb unemployment and launch export-led industrialization gave way temporarily in the early 1980s to the need for higher-skilled activities. The mechanisms of wage determination also changed over time (see the section "Labor market institutions" in chapter 4). One constant, however, has been emphasis on efficient labor allocation. Wages and employment have been largely determined by supply and demand conditions in the market, not by government intervention or pressure from organized labor. The government resisted intervening in the labor market on workers' behalf. The public sector did not act as an employer of last resort or give in to pressure to create low productivity jobs. Singapore has no legal minimum wage with its attendant risk of aggravating unemployment of marginal or inexperienced workers and danger that companies lose competitiveness and depart Singapore. The absence of unemployment compensation has encouraged workers to take a lower-paying job rather than be unemployed, thereby diffusing useful skills through the economy and contributing to low unemployment rates. Differentiating Singapore from some other countries, unions cannot unilaterally raise wages for their members at the expense of others in society. The labor market is integrated. There is no segmentation between a small group of relatively well-paid unionized workers and a large group who are unemployed or pushed into the informal sector.

Wage policy, supported by institutions and attitudes made a key contribution to the proximate sources of economic growth. It was an important factor behind investment and led to high demand for increasingly better qualified labor. Employment was created through market-based growth. Flexible wages that responded to demand for labor resulted in limited layoffs during economic downturns and quick resumption of economic growth. The flexible market for labor facilitated making optimal use of the educational skills of the available human capital. Employee turnover in the MNCs, combined with labor mobility, spread knowledge more widely in the economy, resulting in spill-over of the benefits of FDI.

Flexible wages have contributed to efficient allocation. Flexibility is now increasingly built-in since a portion of total compensation varies automatically with the performance of the economy and the individual enterprise.[35] An efficient, flexible, responsive labor market communicates information about relative costs. It allocates labor according to market forces and exerts competitive discipline. This allowed rapid matching of skills and needs. Sectors that grew fastest had higher wages and higher productivity. Resource allocation improved across firms and industries and thereby contributed to economic growth.

Impressive results followed. Unemployment fell from over 10 percent in 1965 to under 2 percent in the 1990s. Workers were protected through economic growth and job creation. Wages were pulled up by demand forces, not pushed up by government legislation or union pressure. Average real wage growth was close to 5 percent per year in 1973–1997.[36] The upward trend itself facilitated flexibility, resulting in a virtuous cycle.

Singapore's rational policies implied relying on competition, individual incentives and self-interest, and allowing the market to allocate resources. This is not to say that Singapore embraced laissez-faire or does not intervene; simply, that the price mechanism is relied upon for allocation more than in other societies. It has been a source of efficiency, as illustrated in smooth traffic flow, low-cost quality healthcare, and open competition and production for the world market. Flexible labor markets also contributed to efficient allocation. The USSR had high savings but low real growth, illustrating the importance of allocative efficiency of investment.

---

35 In 1987, a system of earlier quantitative guidelines was gradually replaced by a flexi-wage system under which wages are tiered into: a basic component; an annual supplement of one month's basic wage, which could be adjusted in exceptional circumstances; and a variable performance bonus of up to two months' wage based on company performance, as measured by profits or productivity.

36 Real wage growth fell to 2.7 percent on average in 1998–2005, reflecting the need for firms to remain competitive in the face of several adverse shocks including the aftermath of the 1997–98 Asian crisis, the September 11, 2001 terrorist attack, and the SARS epidemic of 2003.

Social Policies for Human Capital Formation

The harshness of market-based competition was compensated by giving people opportunities to participate in economic growth. Better healthcare, education and on-the-job training equipped men and women for gainful employment. Unemployment has been remarkably low. Singapore created new employment opportunities on an ongoing basis, as many of the jobs of the early 1970s have gone to lower-cost neighboring countries. High employment and rising productivity in a growing economy resulted in steadily rising real wage and income growth.

Education and on-the-job training

Investment in human capital through education and on-the-job training were central to this policy. Singapore emphasizes that its people are its only resource. Secondary school enrollment doubled between 1960 and 1965 to prepare the workforce in basic mathematics and science, and vocational schools were opened. The government provided large education and training subsidies. It emphasized the enormous opportunities for all to achieve their potential, regardless of the income status of their parents, through scholarships and access to learning opportunities, tapping the talents for society of all, including poor bright children. Singapore proudly presents many examples of impressive upward mobility. The genuine prospect for advancement of one's children was an important element during wage negotiations in persuading organized labor to temper their earlier militancy.

In the late 1960s, the government began to run the educational system on managerial (as opposed to academic or collegiate) principles, aimed at maximizing medium-term economic growth. The twin objectives were: to produce the skilled artisans and technicians Singapore needed for industrial growth, and to avoid turning out unemployable white-collar graduates. Access to education was rationed through a competitive and strictly merit-based system. Students are channeled into areas according to their capabilities. Some went to polytechnics to meet the rapidly rising need for applied engineering and accounting. Up until the mid-1980s there was no appreciable broadening of education: only 10 percent of those aged 20–24 attended polytechnics or universities. The small number allowed high expenditure per student, contributing to quality education. Less-academically oriented students followed technical and vocational courses. Only after 1985 did higher education become widely available. Rapid economic growth itself created more resources for education. In addition, declining population growth limited the school-age population, thus allowing more resources per pupil. High standards prevail and hard work is expected. English language education for all has helped to expand opportunities. Singapore avoided training substantial numbers in the liberal arts, who would then likely join the ranks of the educated unemployed. Carefully planned government intervention provided optimal technical support and held in check the supply-driven and inappropriate educational mix often found in developing countries.[37]

Education became closely integrated with industrial policy. Firms setting up operations in Singapore needed employees skilled in managing complex assembly operations and precision engineering. On-the-job training took on major importance. MNCs worked closely with the government, trade unions, and employees to organize training programs geared to their particular needs and attended by technically capable employees they themselves selected. The government provided fiscal benefits to MNCs for participating in industrial training centers. Employees benefited from receiving technical training from global industry leaders. Training was specific, targeted to be complementary to the physical capital brought by the MNCs and thus assuring excellent use of educational funds from a growth perspective. Yet, training was sufficiently general to allow employees to switch successfully to more demanding jobs over time.

37 Huff (1999), p. 41.

Zeiss, a German optical precision instrument company, trained 4,000 staff in Singapore. When the firm succumbed to competitive Japanese innovation, many of its well-trained staff were hired by Seagate to start disk-drive production.[38]

Educational opportunities were broad-based. The educational system has shown no bias against females, enhancing their subsequent participation in the labor market. By 1999, females made up 43 percent of the two public sector universities. Nonetheless, as elsewhere, children of less-educated parents are at disadvantage in school. Deliberate efforts were made to improve the school results of the Malay minority, whose preference for religion-based education and a larger number of children per family had set them back. The availability of broad-based opportunities contrasts with countries such as Pakistan, where girls in rural areas often have inadequate access to quality education.

Shared growth through asset redistribution

The PAP started as a socialist party. It withdrew from the Socialist International in 1976 under threat by the Dutch Labor Party of eviction on the grounds of suppression of independent labor unions and freedom of the press. But it believed in sharing economic growth fairly. Led by moderates such as Lee Kuan Yew, its socialism was non-ideological. Its rational approach turned it away from radical socialist income redistribution policies. It disliked the cost of high marginal income and profit tax rates that tend to undermine work ethic and employment creation. The PAP was averse to the dependency culture of recipients of transfers for social welfare or unemployment, wary of undermining the fabric of society and convinced that the alternative of creating broad-based opportunities for people to participate in economic growth was superior. Safety-net support within the family or

38 Retraining of workers helps to overcome resistance against modern technology. Those whose livelihood would be destroyed by a new technology have often tried to block it. French textile workers in the 19th century threw their wooden shoes (*sabot*) in the weaving and spinning machines, reportedly coining the word "sabotage."

through voluntary organizations is preferred. The government's emphasis was on equalizing ex-ante opportunities, not ex-post outcomes. Periodic redistribution of accumulated fiscal surpluses does take place, but mainly in the form of asset enhancement, to top up CPF accounts, provide assistance in enhancing equity in housing, or distribute shares of privatized companies. When shares in Singapore Telecommunications were floated in 1993, the government offered a large portion for sale at half the market value to all adult citizens.

One somewhat surprising redistributive feature in the tradition of radical socialism came as a sideeffect of Singapore's land policy. The Land Acquisition Act (1966) enables the government to secure land needed for public facilities such as schools, hospitals, housing and infrastructure development including roads, drains, and the Mass Rapid Transit system. Under this act, land owned by the state and its statutory boards has risen to about 90 percent of the total from around 40 percent in 1960. In addition to obtaining land released by the British military, the state captured part of the rising value of Singapore's land from individual owners by acquiring land at below market prices. In the late 1970s the government amended the law so as to gain the power to acquire land for public purposes at its value on an earlier date, then fixed at November 30, 1973. Private landowners, it was reasoned, should not profit from an increase in land value brought about by economic development and the infrastructure paid for with public funds.[39] Thereafter, the base year was periodically moved closer as market prices continued to rise. The government leases the land in its possession for residential, commercial, and industrial development for a period up to 99 years.[40] The revenue from these leases allows tax rates to be lower than they otherwise would be. This form of wealth redistribution did not create the disincentives of income redistribution.

---

39 Lee Kuan Yew (2000), p. 119.

40 As pointed out by Huff (1999), p. 40, Singapore followed economic theory, which indicates that in a world of mobile capital and perfect information, a small country should not tax capital, but immobile factors of production such as land and labor.

Socially inspired policies in Singapore paid off most in public housing.[41] From 1960 to 1980, the HDB built almost 400,000 apartments at an accelerating pace. Large numbers moved from slum and squatter areas into these apartments which they initially rented but subsequently purchased from the HDB. With income levels rising over time, owners moved to bigger HDB units, including executive apartments and condominiums. By 2005, more than 88 percent of the resident population lived in government-built housing and 93 percent owned their homes. The government heavily subsidized mortgage loans and the purchase price of HDB flats up to specified income levels.

Home ownership was believed to enhance commitment to defend the country and being important for national unity. With a mortgage to service, people have to work and save. The roof above their head turned uncommitted footloose tenants into responsible home owners, with beneficial effects for the neighborhood as home ownership became stakeholdership. Housing units formed the basis for neighborhood community councils that served as government-linked grassroots organizations. With a view to strengthening mutual family support, the government gives housing grants to the newly married provided they choose to live within a close range to their parents. Bloc ethnic limits discourage racial and religious concentration and encourage ethnic dispersion and diversity.

As noted by Linda Low, Japan, South Korea, and Taiwan carried through radical land reforms under strong governments. This laid the groundwork for equality of opportunity and economic growth in these countries. By contrast, land reform in the Philippines failed under American-style democracy after 1945 and feudal power persists. In Singapore, the public housing program was in some ways equivalent to land reform. It can be called a "microcosm of government-made Singapore."[42]

---

41 The discussion of the housing program in this section draws on Linda Low (1998).
42 Low (1998), pp. 3, 181, and 240.

Effective policy design

Policies in Singapore heeded budgeting discipline, relied on price incentives, and created opportunities to participate in economic growth. In addition, policies were well designed. The government addressed the principal binding constraints as they evolved over time, adapted policies to changing conditions and local circumstances, and reversed course when policy mistakes had occurred. Policies were carefully crafted, coherent, and credible. There was not from the beginning a grand overall design for the next 40 years, but basic principles from which policies evolved.

Addressing binding constraints

As emphasized recently in the development literature, countries must find ways to channel private investment into new non-traditional activities to create a succession of successful growth episodes. Otherwise, growth will peter out.[43] Schumpeter identified this process of creation of new industries and destruction of old ones as an essential feature of capitalism.[44] By addressing binding constraints, economic policies facilitate the emergence of new profitable activities.

Singapore's development history illustrates this process of moving into higher value-added activities as a way of raising productivity, resulting in continual structural transformation. Whereas in some countries governments limit themselves to creating a climate conducive for private entrepreneurship to ignite, the Singapore government proactively engineers the various successions, spearheading restructuring sequentially, including through the state enterprise system.

The shrinking of the internal market following separation from Malaysia rendered the import-substitution strategy, which Singapore had pursued briefly, no longer viable. Soon the city-state returned to its long tradition as a free port and the advantages of open inter-

43 Rodrik (2004); Hausmann et al. (2004).
44 Schumpeter J. (1947).

national markets that had made entrepôt trade profitable. Accordingly, during *1967–73*, Singapore opted for *export-oriented industrialization*, which focused on production of labor-intensive, low value-added items such as textiles, garments, furniture, electrical household appliances, ship repair, and simple repetitive assembly tasks in consumer electronics. Subsequently, capital intensity increased with investments in petroleum refining and chemicals.

The binding constraint during this period was insufficient indigenous entrepreneurship to create jobs for the large numbers of low-skilled unemployed. Creating the conditions that would persuade MNCs to locate in Singapore was key. The newly established Jurong Town Corporation developed and managed industrial estates and offered ready-made factories. In 1967, tax incentives were introduced to promote exports. Legislation introduced in 1968 fostered harmonious labor relations and wage moderation helped absorb unemployment. MNCs benefited from government-provided infrastructure. The early 1970s also saw a rapidly expanding public housing program that created jobs and contributed to social stability.

The *1973–84* period targeted *economic restructuring with technological catch-up*. The achievement of full employment exerted upward pressure on wages. Staying competitive internationally required upgrading of exports. Investments in skill- and technology-intensive sectors, including electronics, computers, precision engineering, machinery, and pharmaceuticals became important to generate higher value-added per worker. Policies supported this transition: tax holidays during this phase favored investment in skill-intensive activities.[45] The binding constraint became skilled labor for

45 Singapore made extensive use of profit tax exemptions for selected industries under various schemes that were administered by the EDB. These included the Pioneer Industries Ordinance and the Industrial Expansion Ordinance of 1959 and the Economic Expansion Incentives Act of 1967. Tax relief was conditional on performance: it applied to specific investments or to income streams specifically attributed to certain products or to exports. The World Bank (1993) emphasized this conditionality as key to the relative success of industrial policies in the East Asian Miracle economies.

higher valued-added exports. Subsidized industrial training centers set up jointly with the MNCs built engineering skills. To encourage enterprises to opt for automation, a levy on foreign unskilled labor was introduced in 1978, wage increases in excess of productivity were in fact encouraged, and the employer contribution to the CPF was raised to 25 percent of wages by 1984.

During *1985–1997* Singapore aimed for *economic diversification*, sector-wise and geographically. The 1985 recession exposed the danger of excessive concentration of exports in a few sectors such as electronics and chemicals. Singapore had to develop and be competitive in a wider spectrum of activities. In services, the focus turned to leveraging the city-state's locational advantage and trade expertise to successfully develop air transportation, telecommunications, logistics, shipping, and cargo handling facilities. Business and financial services were further expanded, building on the offshore market first started in 1968. An Asian dollar bond market was also engineered by the government and after 1985, there was focus on building up a domestic asset management industry to reduce dependence on New York. By 1993, Singapore hosted 115 foreign banks. The 1990s saw growing emphasis on conference facilities as self-contained business centers. Biotechnological and other MNCs were enticed to locate their regional headquarters and R&D facilities to Singapore. Business and financial services grew to one-fourth of GDP. Meanwhile, industrialization moved up to capital- and skill-intensive higher value-added activities such as precision instruments, complex aspects of disk-drive design, and pharmaceuticals. Policies again supported the transition: the government expanded educational facilities for more students over longer years. Also, to further reduce vulnerability, Singapore sought a second source of income by helping its own companies develop and expand elsewhere into the region.

In the *period after the 1997–98* Asian financial crisis, Singapore further evolved into an advanced and globally competitive *knowledge-*

intensive economy.[46] Ongoing restructuring aims to ensure long-term competitiveness. Chemical, biochemical, and pharmaceutical industries are aimed at decreasing the dependence on the volatile IT capital expenditure cycle with its declining margins. Within electronics and chemicals, there was constant upgrading to more demanding tasks. Singapore moved to become an innovation center of higher learning, business education and opportunities, venture capital, engineering design, software development, and most recently, media studios and wastewater recycling and purification technology and reverse osmosis-based desalination plants. Singapore aims to become a key node in a global network of people and ideas. Digital and interactive media has started with the arrival of firms such as Lucasfilm and is expected to generate 3 percent of GDP by 2018. Environmental and water purification technology and the biomedical industry are expected to create 40,000 new jobs by 2015. Emphasis is placed on marketing and design services and on making Singapore a choice location for international events. The intention is also to develop Singapore into Asia's regional private banking fund management, medical, education, intellectual property protection, and tourism hub. Policies support this latest transition through several measures, as follows: Singapore developed its arts scene and other amenities to attract foreign professionals and skilled workers.

Concerned about dependence on regional markets, Singapore encouraged its companies to locate beyond ASEAN and Asia and for Singapore firms to form global alliances and compete on the world stage. To underpin rapid trade growth, a series of bilateral free trade and Comprehensive Economic Cooperation Agreements (CECAs)

46 The Asian financial crisis was triggered in July 1997 with the devaluation of the Thai baht under intense speculative pressure. The crisis then spread to South Korea and Indonesia, leading to sharp declines in currencies, stock markets, and output. It threatened these countries' financial systems and triggered large contractions in output, disrupting many lives. Singapore's financial fundamentals enabled it to weather the crisis quite well.

were concluded with several countries including New Zealand (2000), Japan (2002), Australia (2003), the United States (2003), India (2005), and South Korea (2005) to complement Singapore's ongoing efforts at regional and multilateral trade liberalization. Emphasis shifted further to creativity, innovation, and entrepreneurship as new sources of productivity growth.

Many countries have designed elaborate economic policy strategies with structural reform programs that address a wide range of issues. Often, however, these programs fail to focus on the most binding constraint, mainly for political reasons. Consequently, their growth performance has turned out to be disappointing. Rather than trying to address all areas at the same time, better results can be expected if governments diagnose the most binding constraint their economy confronts at any given moment. Searching for a lost car-key at night in the light of a nearby street lamp, regardless of where the key was lost in the first place, but "because that is where the light shines" will not likely start the engine. The Singapore government focused on overcoming the most important current obstacles to growth as they evolved over time in a sequence of targeted reforms, as each decade threw up new challenges.

Growth resulted in a rapidly changing composition on the production side, in part spurred by the gathering forces of regional and global competition that buffeted Singapore's highly open economy. Globalization itself had been stimulated, as the successful strategies of Singapore and other high-performing East Asian economies found imitation elsewhere. Singapore demonstrated nimble adaptability and resilience in response to shifting comparative advantage, with the economy steadily moving up the value ladder, taking full advantage of what the MNCs had to offer. Economic policies helped facilitate this succession of transitions.

Pragmatic policy adaptation and correction

Policies were adapted and even reversed as circumstances changed. The government was risk-averse and deliberately very careful.

Starting in 1959, the government did not discard Singapore's British heritage, but preserved and improved upon what it considered to be useful. There was no policy blueprint for the next 40 years, but there were core values that did not change. The government has been creative and innovative, but also flexible, in many policy areas. In the 1960s, the government urged couples, and provided financial incentives, to limit the number of children to two per family. When the sharp drop in the fertility rate resulted in labor shortages and an older growing population by 1986, the government switched to a pro-natalist course—some say belatedly. The previous "Stop at two" birth-control policy was replaced by encouragement of "three or more children per family, if the parents have the means to provide education and quality upbringing." Education policies have also changed pragmatically over the years,[47] so did transportation and healthcare policies as discussed earlier.

Occasionally, policies failed to work as intended. When policies had been misjudged or miscalculated, the government took action by reversing its course. One of those rare instances took place in the early 1980s when the "wage correction policy" had itself to be corrected. During 1973–80, the policy of keeping wages in hand encouraged an influx of foreign workers with low value-added productivity. This did not prompt industry restructuring. Starting in 1979, the government corrected the artificially low-wage policy by in fact encouraging wage increases in excess of productivity growth in the expectation that this would spur firms to move rapidly into more capital-intensive and higher value-added activities. The high-wage policy of 1979 was meant to orchestrate belated economic restructuring. Firms' response time, however, was slower than had been expected. Although the policy succeeded in encouraging employers to restructure, labor costs, particularly CPF contributions, rose rapidly and for so long, that the loss of competitiveness eventually became a problem.[48] This aggravated the 1985 recession,

47 Mauzy and Milne (2002), p. 104.
48 Bercuson (1995), p. 30.

and the initial policy was subsequently abandoned, in favor of substantial cuts in CPF rates and the abolition or reduction in employment taxes. In 2005, the government decided to build integrated resorts, reversing the long-standing policy on casinos. In a small city-state, there is little margin for error, and policies must be designed to address changing circumstances.

Policies tailored to local conditions

The design of monetary and exchange rate policy since 1980 is a case in point.[49] By that time, exchange controls had been progressively dismantled and Singapore was fully integrated in global capital markets: arbitrage flows meant that Singapore could set the nominal level of either the domestic interest rate or the exchange rate, but not both.

The extreme openness of the trade account convinced the authorities to operate monetary policy through changes in the nominal exchange rate as an intermediate target, with domestic price stability as the ultimate objective. The pervasiveness of imported goods throughout the economy means that, to a high degree, domestic prices in Singapore are equivalent to international prices multiplied by the exchange rate. Under these conditions a policy-induced nominal appreciation of the Singapore dollar has a powerful downward impact on domestic prices and costs, enabling the MAS to neutralize imported inflation. Equally important, a policy to deliberately weaken the currency to stimulate exports is unlikely to be effective given the strong pass-through from import prices to domestic prices and wages. Singapore instead relied on productivity improvements to maintain competitiveness.

Singapore has a hybrid exchange rate regime that combines features of three different systems. The Singapore dollar is a floating currency, as in a flexible exchange rate regime, but only within an undisclosed band. The MAS enters—and dominates—the foreign

49 Monetary Authority of Singapore (2003); Parrado (2004).

exchange market, on the demand or supply side as might be required, to keep the rate from exiting the band—the defining feature of a fixed exchange rate regime. Finally, as in a managed regime, the MAS periodically sets the band in light of current and prospective inflation pressure. If foreign inflation—or to a lesser extent domestic unit labor costs in response to strong economic growth—threaten to boost inflation to unacceptable levels, the exchange rate band will be raised to allow a nominal currency appreciation and thus maintain domestic price stability. Although the exchange rate is typically quoted in U.S. dollar terms, the MAS monitors the rate of the Singapore dollar and formulates its policy in terms of an undisclosed trade-weighted basket of currencies

Official intervention in the foreign exchange market keeps the rate within the band. If speculative capital inflows threaten excessive appreciation, the MAS steps in to add to its stock of official foreign reserves by selling Singapore dollars. Equally, the drain on domestic liquidity caused by the high savings in the form of budget surpluses or large CPF contributions may lead the MAS to accommodate demand for Singapore dollars by purchasing foreign exchange to add to its official reserves.

This carefully engineered system has served Singapore well. All along, the real exchange rate remained competitive as Singapore largely avoided the overvaluation that characterized fixed exchange rate regimes that suffered domestic inflation. In the wake of the Asian financial crisis, the prevailing regime allowed the Singapore dollar to depreciate against the U.S. dollar and other major currencies, yet appreciate against the currencies of neighboring countries that were deeply devalued, including by widening the band. Domestic inflation remained stable and international confidence in Singapore's monetary management was preserved. Unorthodox cost-cutting (see the section "Purposeful state intervention" later in this chapter) was probably essential to complement exchange rate policy.

Coherent and predictable

Quite a few countries have disappointing economic growth results because of policy incoherence. Daran Acemoglu refers to a "seesaw" effect: the beneficial impact of one policy action that "uplifts" the economy is undone by an offsetting measure in another policy area that "depresses" the economy.[50] Some countries opened up to international trade by lowering import duties but failed to recover the lost budgetary revenue by broadening the domestic tax base. Others allowed artificially suppressed domestic interest rates to find their market-determined equilibrium without taking into account the higher cost of servicing the government debt. Another example is carrying out needed fiscal adjustment by cutting investment in priority infrastructure or basic health and education outlays. This is a risk for governments that are committed to large entitlement programs such as income transfers, untargeted subsidies, and excessive public sector employment.

Singapore's development experience, by contrast, shows many instances of policies that were highly coherent. They were carefully engineered to be mutually reinforcing, creating virtuous cycles.[51]

First, FDI inflow, disciplined and flexible wage policy, employment creation, education, and the resulting economic growth itself are all closely intertwined in mutually reinforcing causality going in multiple directions. Thus, FDI was possible, thanks to the wage and education policies. It created employment and economic growth, which in turn supported non-confrontational labor relations. Steadily rising real wages and worker access to low-cost housing and education contributed to political and industrial peace and held down wage demands, which in turn fostered macroeconomic stability. Because growth and employment were achieved, there was no obvious antipathy to foreign capital and labor.

50 Acemoglu et al. (2004).

51 Turning vicious circles into virtuous cycles is a long-established concept in development economics and has also been highlighted by Professor Lim Chong Yah (2004), p. 366, who coined it the Cumulative Causation Theory.

Second, low domestic inflation supported international competitiveness, enabling the government to borrow at a low cost through the CPF and persuading CPF participants to trust that the purchasing power of their accumulated savings would not be eroded. It created confidence in the value of the Singapore dollar, allowed the financial sector to develop, and was instrumental in maintaining wage discipline. Macroeconomic stability provided strong fundamentals allowing unrestricted access to foreign exchange and profit repatriation.

Policies were predictable and credible because they were coherent. Terms of trade declines via oil shocks were addressed through the adjustment of expenditure to the lower disposable income. Financing was confined to drawing down a limited portion of assets built up through earlier saving, and not by incurring indebtedness. Hence, the economy bounced back rapidly and investors maintained their confidence. There was a remarkable degree of continuity in major principles and outlines of strategy since 1965, yet important changes took place pragmatically in response to an evolving international environment. Policies were politically sustainable owing to partnership and mutual trust between the government and key economic players. The remarkable adaptability and resilience to external shocks or new challenges fed on itself, with success breeding success.

FOUR BASIC PRINCIPLES

Singapore's policy framework was a key factor behind the country's superior growth performance. Four broad principles have been identified: (i) fiscal discipline helped generate savings and formed the basis of macroeconomic stability that inspired confidence; (ii) the use of price incentives in key areas such as healthcare, transportation, and the labor market, and integration with world markets promoted efficient resource allocation; (iii) opportunities for participating in economic growth were created and shared widely among the population by raising people's productivity through better health, education, and housing; and (iv) policies were well designed. They facilitated dynamic restructuring by removing binding constraints on private investment in newly profitable activities, adapted to changing conditions over time, took local circumstances into account, and were highly coherent. All four principles, applied across a range of policies, helped achieve high factor accumulation and productivity increase, which in Singapore's case centered on inflows of foreign direct investment.

The four broad principles of policy we have highlighted, and illustrated in Singapore's specific case, provide useful benchmarks for other countries to assess their own economic policies for their contribution to economic growth. While the extent and magnitude, for example of saving, can be debated, the principles themselves are sufficiently general to be uncontroversial.[52] Another key element of Singapore's economic policies to which we now turn is less generally applicable.

PURPOSEFUL STATE INTERVENTION

In Singapore, the state and not the local private sector, has been the driver for development. The invisible hand that serves the common good through self-interest is guided by the strong visible arm of the government through benevolent state involvement.[53] There was not a blind market fundamentalism or laissez-faire. Instead, the government worked with the market: it did not ignore or command it. Goh Keng Swee, Singapore's original economic architect saw no contradiction between expousing free-market principles and advocating efficient state intervention when required. The PAP government intervened heavily across the economy. It planned the country's long-term strategic development as if it were a corporation.

52 The pace of government-led restructuring could be too quick. Young (1992) attributed the low TFP in Singapore to the premature introduction of advanced physical capital under the government's incentives program before labor was ready and before the older technology had yielded its full benefit.

53 Low (1998), p. 23.

Major economic planning exercises, starting in 1960 with the visit of Dr Albert Winsemius and periodically repeated thereafter, provided the framework for the economic policies. Task forces and economic advisory committees sprinkled the 40-year period, producing specific quantitative targets. Policies were methodically derived to solve specific problems. Quantitative targets to be reached at future points in time served as benchmarks to allow monitoring if policies were on track. The TFP debate in the mid-1980s gave birth to a new committee, explicitly charged with ensuring that TFP growth would reach 2 percent annually at least. In 2002, a plan to develop the life sciences specified as a goal that "at least 15 world-class companies" would establish their regional headquarters in Singapore by 2010, which is remarkable specific targeting.

Three aspects can be distinguished.

Entrepreneurial role

First, the state itself assumed an entrepreneurial role through public enterprises. The state acted as both agenda-setter and agenda-achiever.[54] An important part of Singapore's economic activity is conducted by statutory boards and GLCs, estimated to number in the hundreds.[55] In addition, the government commands the use of large amounts of CPF savings. The government has used GLCs in its efforts

54 Low (1998), Preface.

55 GLCs are government-controlled companies that reside under a statutory board or under one of four holdings, with Temasek Holdings being the largest in terms of assets. Statutory boards are de facto extensions of the civil service. They are supervised by ministries and accountable to Parliament, but enjoy autonomy in their day-to-day operations. It is estimated that GLCs contributed 13 percent of Singapore's GDP in the late 1990s (Source: Peebles and Wilson (2002), p. 14). By end-March 2005, Temasek Holdings had built up a portfolio worth S$103 billion. (Source: http://www.temasekholdings.com.sg/2005review.) About half of its assets are located in Singapore, a ratio Temasek intends to lower to one third, while raising its shareholdings in the rest of Asia to one-third of the total. It has bought banks, shopping malls, container shipping facilities and pharmaceuticals in China, hotels and senior citizen homes in Britain and Germany, and telecommunications facilities in Bangladesh. Temasek is the controlling shareholder of seven of Singapore's 10 biggest companies, including Singapore Telecommunications Ltd (SingTel) and Singapore Airlines Ltd (SIA).

to diversify away from entrepôt trade to sectors such as shipbuilding, banking, and electronics. It has also used them as a counterweight to Singapore's dependence on MNCs, while stressing their independent management. Many GLCs, such as Singapore Airlines, are listed on the stock exchange, being partly in private hands. Among the major statutory boards, the Jurong Town Corporation played a pioneering role in building and managing industrial, commercial, and science-oriented premises, thus providing support to incoming MNCs. The Public Utilities Board (PUB), the Port of Singapore Authority (PSA) and the HDB played a key role.

Singapore shared with many developing and advanced countries the heavy role of the state in a wide range of economic activities, which was not unusual until some 25 years ago. In Singapore, like in many other countries, public enterprises have since been progressively privatized. Often, however, public enterprises elsewhere failed to display the profitability, budgetary discipline, and dynamism found in Singapore, where GLCs have not been used for social or employment generation purposes. Many GLCs have consistently posted strong financial performances. Among the best known and most profitable companies in Singapore are GLCs, such as Singapore Airlines, Singapore Telecommunications, DBS Bank, Keppel Corporation, and SembCorp Industries. A public report on Temasek Holdings, one of the government's four holding companies, revealed a total shareholder's return of 18 percent per annum over the past 31 years, although due partly to the Asian financial crisis and stock market fluctuations, returns have been lower over the past 5–10 years.[56] Singapore Airlines has long been ranked among the most admired companies in the world. Its success is derived from meritocratic management and operation of the company on firm commercial principles as an autonomous profit-seeking entity. At one point, the government threatened to close down the enterprise if management and unions failed to cooperate, stressing the importance of profitability.

---

56 See http://www.temasekholdings.com.sg/2005review/.

Selective intervention

A second aspect is selective intervention. Singapore, while highly open to foreign capital, has nonetheless steered it selectively. The state played a key role, beyond facilitation, in guiding private investment in strategic directions. The main instruments have been various tax concessions and fiscal incentives, including exemptions from profit tax for 5–10 years, and the provision of land at subsidized prices for specific activities. The economic rationale for these concessions was that foreign direct investors would create additional benefits for Singapore that were not likely to be reflected in their own profits. Favorable externalities included substantial spillover of knowledge across firms, clusters of specialized local firms that would become suppliers to MNCs or enter joint ventures with them, and opportunities for capturing dynamic economies of scale that result from learning.

How did industrial policy in Singapore sidestep the pitfalls that have trapped other countries? First, tax concessions granted did not undermine government revenue, given the strong fiscal position. In addition, the EDB entered joint ventures with some foreign investors, acquiring a share of the profits. This has benefited Singapore's budget. Second, concessions were conditional upon performance: already in 1967, Singapore sharply reduced the corporate income tax rate on approved manufacturers' profits from 40 percent to 4 percent for 15 years, provided the manufactured goods were exported: companies had to meet the test of the international market. Third, the development track to which the MNCs were invited—which emphasized labor-intensive production initially, capital deepening, and technological upgrading subsequently, and diversification thereafter—was consistent with Singapore's evolving comparative advantages.[57] Capital-intensive production conformed to market realities. Fourth, the number of promoted projects that went awry

57 This was emphasized in World Bank (1993).

appears to have been relatively small.[58] This high success rate may in part reflect the nature of the political system, which has ensured that rent-seeking activities have not determined which firms or sectors receive favorable treatment.[59] Singapore's deliberate steps to stimulate new growth sectors have worked. Since 2000, the biomedical sector has grown rapidly to become a S$18 billion industry, which contributed 5 percent of GDP in 2005. Picking winners can fail. The government is cautious in providing support, aware of the risks in allocating funds for strategic R&D.

Countercyclical intervention

A third aspect is Singapore's reliance on unusually direct countercyclical intervention methods during times of adverse external demand shocks, such as the 1997 Asian financial crisis. The reason is that monetary policy is impotent and fiscal policy of only limited effectiveness to stimulate demand: the very high import content of local production quickly spills the fiscal stimulus into additional demand—abroad. Singapore, however, has another arrow in its quiver that other countries lack. The government directly intervened to temporarily lower the cost of business in Singapore through its influence over public utilities and its power to lower the CPF contribution rate of employers. These direct intervention methods, as occurred in 1998, helped achieve real cost reductions and reassured the MNCs of the government's commitment to assist them in remaining internationally competitive. Layoffs and recessions were avoided more easily than in other countries.

Elsewhere, substantial nominal currency devaluation is often the last and only resort in the face of downwardly sticky nominal wages, often with higher inflation as an undesirable side effect. In contrast, Singapore used the direct intervention methods at its disposal. In

58 One example is losses incurred by Singapore Technologies related to its acquisition of Micropolis, a hard disk drive company, in 1996 when heavy competition by rivals resulted in losses.

59 Bercuson (1995), p. 19.

addition, there is built-in wage flexibility, because an important portion of workers' remuneration is automatically lowered if GDP growth falls short of target. Consequently, Singapore experienced a smaller depreciation of its currency than would otherwise have been required—a favorable result since nominal currency depreciation is quickly undone by rising import prices in a highly open economy and can undermine investor confidence. The direct intervention methods helped put Singapore's economy back on its growth track by the middle of 1999.[60]

State intervention in many other countries has failed to work in the absence of sound basic principles, such as budgetary discipline, efficient market-based allocation, a competent civil service, and sharing opportunities for economic growth widely. A government role in investment policy need not preclude sustained growth if it supports efficient, export-oriented development. Planning need not always be a failure. By most accounts, state intervention in Singapore has functioned remarkably well.

The rapid growth of GLCs and statutory boards has led, however, to a different concern, namely that they encroach upon too many non-strategic industries, crowding out smaller private companies and hindering the development of a critical mass of thriving local companies.[61] A different criticism sometimes voiced contends that they do worse than private sector firms because their managers are mainly civil servants who lack business acumen or adequate risk appetite.

---

60 The reverse of these direct intervention measures occurred in the first half of the 1980s: high wage agreements were met with rising CPF contribution rates in part to siphon off excess liquidity.

61 Ramirez and Tan (2004) found that investors assign a premium to GLCs over private companies. They demonstrated that GLCs enjoy a higher market value relative to book value (a ratio James Tobin, 1981 Nobel laureate in Economics, labeled *q*) than is the case with private companies listed in Singapore. After controlling for the variables that typically explain *q* such as the price-to-earnings ratio, debt-to-equity ratio, and company size, Ramirez and Tan concluded that capital markets seem to reward the very fact that a company is linked to the government, possibly because of "brand recognition" or because investors may believe, rightly or wrongly, that the Singapore government protects GLCs from failure.

Four Growth-enhancing Institutions and Culture

Institutions—The Foundation of Singapore's prosperity

Underlying Singapore's impressive growth performance is a set of institutions that have facilitated the design and implementation of sound growth-oriented policies. By permitting good policies, institutions have promoted the proximate causes of economic growth discussed in Chapter 1. In addition, solid public institutions have fostered a favorable climate for investment, which has directly contributed to factor accumulation, technological progress, and efficiency gains.

Institutions in support of policy implementation

Governments have often formulated pro-growth economic development strategies, but failed to implement them. Many countries, like Singapore, also *designed* policies that aimed at fiscal consolidation, efficient market-based allocation, building human capital, and dynamic allocation to new sectors with higher-growth potential, as well as coherent policies that mutually reinforce each other, turning vicious circles into virtuous cycles. Yet, unlike Singapore, policies often were not implemented, were reversed soon after their introduction, or had their beneficial impact undone by new measures that counteracted. Sustained coherent policy *implementation* failed for lack of underpinning by pro-growth institutions. Singapore's economic prowess over many other countries reflects superior planning—and execution.

Inadequate institutions impeded economic growth in many countries by not allowing implementation of sound macroeconomic and structural policies. A poorly functioning civil service, including at the local government level, often resulted in non-implementation of policies that are associated with high growth, such as fiscal consolidation. Lacking efficient and honest government, countries failed to develop effective education, health, and labor market systems for a productive and competitive workforce or to promote strong banking systems and capital markets that contribute to economic growth.

Often, non-implementation of pro-growth policies is attributed to lack of "political will." Persistence, despite good policy intentions, of high rates of inflation, loss-making public enterprises, cumbersome red tape that makes the establishment of new firms costly and time consuming, or inflexible labor markets, is taken as evidence that the authorities lack "ownership" of pro-growth policies. However, underlying poor policy implementation is often a malfunctioning social contract about what constitutes fair distribution of the gains and losses from economic progress. Superficial consensus in support of vague principles often masks fundamental discord within society about the perceived distribution of the costs and benefits of economic growth. Policies remain unimplemented because the laborious task of persuading public opinion, the media, and the elite has not led to fruition. Why were good policies implemented in Singapore that fizzled elsewhere?

Douglas North, who won the Noble Prize for Economic Sciences in 1993, defined institutions as the "rules of the game" that set incentives and shape the behavior of organizations and individuals in society.[1] Institutions can be formal rules, such as a country's constitution, laws, regulations, and internal procedures. Or they can be informal values and norms, such as those that drive bureaucratic behavior. Institutions are man-made and rooted in history. They set the incentives that enable societies to organize and function in an orderly way, including through contracts. Sound institutions create

1 North (1991), p. 97.

the collective understanding that is necessary to permit implementation of rational policies in support of sustained economic growth. Institutions are the mechanism of governance.

Effective institutions contribute directly to economic growth

Institutions, thus defined, also contribute directly to factor accumulation and productivity enhancement. Respect for property rights, an impartial judiciary, and adherence to the rule of law all foster investment. Growth-sustaining institutions such as these ensure access to the return for offering one's labor and capital by protecting against predation by the state and others. In the absence of such institutions, fear of losing these rewards discourages investment in physical and human capital and labor contribution.

Pro-growth institutions also allow individuals and enterprises to take advantage of the potential offered by technological progress or international trade liberalization.[2] Good institutions such as flexible labor markets, entry and exit rules for enterprises, and access to credit and knowledge allow individuals and firms to take advantage of market opportunities. Without sound institutions, rapid restructuring of the economy to higher value-added activities and the resulting productivity improvements are inhibited.

In sum, many low-growth countries lacked the institutions that allow sustained implementation of macroeconomic and structural policies that are conducive to high rates of physical and human capital formation, labor market participation, technological progress, and productivity increases. Good economic policies and institutions are intertwined. Together, they promote the proximate causes of economic growth.

Empirical work by Daran Acemoglu and coauthors claims that differences in "institutions" explain three-quarters of the variation in

2 This theme is developed in World Bank (2002).

the *level* of per capita income found nowadays across different countries.[3] Economically advanced countries tend to have "good" institutions while low-income countries are characterized by "bad" institutions. In the study, the quality of a country's institutions is approximated through quantitative indicators of perceptions of a country's respect for the rule of law and integrity of its public administration. Causality is not unidirectional, however, and feedback occurs from high-income levels to institutions. Nonetheless, econometric techniques that rely on instrumental variables support the importance of institutions as a key determinant of economic growth. The huge disparity in economic growth performance between the two Koreas since 1953 highlights the role of economic policies as shaped by different institutions of government.[4]

Strong institutions behind Singapore's growth

Singapore created durable institutions that made its investment climate among the most business-friendly in Asia. These include: (i) a highly efficient civil service; (ii) respect for the rule of law and protection of property rights; (iii) a high level of public integrity; and (iv) social inclusion leading to political stability

Competent civil service and government

As noted in *The Economist*, Singapore has a reputation for its trademark high-quality administration.[5] The efficient handling of the SARS outbreak in 2003 is a case in point. Its bureaucracy is highly effective.[6] Meritocratic principles govern recruitment and promotion. The civil service enjoys a high status. Its remuneration is competitive with the private sector and wage compression of the salary scale, typical elsewhere, is avoided. Attractive remuneration does not

3 Acemoglu et al. (2004).
4 Weil (2005), p. 332.
5 *The Economist*, March 23, 2006.
6 Staff of statutory boards, although not civil servants, are considered part of the bureaucracy.

burden the government budget since there is no overstaffing and the civil service is kept lean. Singapore has many competent and effective institutions. Over time, these institutions have imbued their younger civil servants with a pragmatic philosophy of highly effective governance.

The Economic Development Board (EDB), the lead agency that plans and executes the government's development strategy, has built a reputation for excellence since its inception in 1961. Its staff played a key role in attracting, negotiating conditions, and coordinating as a one-window-agency for the MNCs that made Singapore their platform for exporting to the world. As recalled by Lee Kuan Yew, even small successes in the early years required exceptional perseverance from EDB staff, given Singapore's dim prospects. Staff, however, were highly motivated to serve the young republic, eager to learn, and had been selected from among the best.[7] Efforts were rewarded when Texas Instruments set up facilities in 1968, followed by National Semiconductor, Hewlett Packard, General Electric, and many others. The strength and professionalism of the EDB was an important institutional link that supported the range of economic policies geared toward attracting FDI to Singapore.[8] It was one consideration that led Seagate to choose Singapore over Hong Kong and South Korea in 1982.

The Monetary Authority of Singapore helped promote strong banking systems and capital markets. Following the granting of a charter to Bank of America in 1968, Singapore steadily developed into an international banking hub, with the financial services sector representing 12 percent of GDP by the late 1990s. Yet, for many years, Singapore had to fight a dogged battle internationally to establish trust in the integrity of its financial system and its capacity to prevent systemic failure. As the supervisory agency, the MAS adopted a cautious approach toward the regulation of the financial sector, insisting on high capital adequacy for banks and carefully

---

7 Lee Kuan Yew (2000), Chapter 4.
8 Schein (1996).

monitoring financial institutions for non-performing assets and compliance with other regulations. Bankers sometimes complained that the top-down guidance stifled private sector innovation, but investors had confidence in the sector's strong prudential oversight. Such pre-emptive surveillance helps explain why Singapore endured the Asian financial crisis of 1997/98 better than its neighbors, with minimal damage to its financial sector.[9]

Few people anywhere pay taxes gladly, and the same can be said for Singapore. Yet, tax compliance is high, as is observance of the rule of law in general. Other features have helped as well: the government justifies responsible allocation of taxpayers' money and follows stringent rules on the expenditure side; income tax rates are low; and the tax administration as well as the customs service are highly professional. Both institutions helped make Singapore's fiscal and open-trade policy unusually successful. That is not to say that systems have been functioning smoothly all along. Problems did exist earlier. By 1991, the tax department faced a huge backlog of income tax assessments that had built up over the years. Staff morale was low because until then the tax administration had to recompute all tax returns, and to compound the problem, the number of returns had grown rapidly along with the economy but civil service rules prevented staff expansion.[10] To rectify the situation, in 1992 the Revenue Department was converted into a statutory board, the Internal Revenue Authority of Singapore (IRAS). The government pays IRAS a fee for its services that is linked to performance. Work processes were restructured with the introduction of self-assessment by taxpayers. Major technical upgrading and automation took place. These efforts helped lift staff morale. The timing of the tax administration reform is interesting. It illustrates that upgrading of institutions is an ongoing process, which is helped by economic growth itself, and that institutional perfection across the board is not a prerequisite for growth to take off.

9 Peebles and Wilson (2000), Chapter 8.
10 Asher (2002), p. 415.

Ezra Vogel contended that, "What is unusual in Singapore is not the prominence of meritocratic administrators, but the fact that meritocracy extends upward to include virtually all political leaders."[11] Indeed, Diane Mauzy and RS Milne give a fascinating account of the rigorous selection process and standards of skill and character adopted by the PAP to select its candidates for Parliament, and eventually ministerial responsibilities, by co-opting talent.[12] The PAP pays extraordinary attention to people's ability to deliver results and promotes or demotes accordingly. Top officials in the government and civil service work closely together and are on the board of directors of GLCs and statutory boards, making for an integrated and hierarchical approach. Cross-directorships in GLCs are a subtle but powerful way in which the state facilitates macroeconomic policy coordination.[13] Although the practice has been criticized, from the PAP's viewpoint, the scarcity of top talent makes inevitable the multiple responsibilities, and resulting fusion. For many years, the chairman of the MAS was also the finance minister, thereby enabling effective coordination. But such a situation also poses a potential conflict of interest, which in other countries might have been a recipe for runaway inflation. In Singapore, however, the fox proved exceptional and the hen-house was well protected.

Labor market institutions

The notion of the government acting as mediator between labor and capital as a means of moderating industrial strife is quite common in Europe. Tripartism found its expression in the International Labor Organization's constitution in 1919 as a means for reconciling the imperatives of social justice with those of enterprise competitiveness and economic development. Singapore institutionalized wage consultations with the creation of the National Wages Council

11 Vogel, (1989), pp. 1052–53.
12 Mauzy and Milne (2002), pp. 48–49.
13 Low (1998), p. 164. Note that links with the state have at times complicated international acquisitions by Singapore's GLCs.

(NWC) in 1972. The NWC was established to provide a framework for orderly wage settlements and to prevent wage bargaining from sparking inflation in a tightening labor market. Comprising representatives of the government, employers, and unions, and headed by a neutral chairman, the council reaches decisions by consensus.[14] Each year, the NWC reviews wage and economic trends before advising the government on wage adjustment guidelines for the different sectors. The guidelines were originally expressed as a single figure but became qualitative from 1987, consistent with the shift to the more market-oriented "flexi-wage" system. The quantitative wage recommendations were never binding, but the public sector consistently adhered to them. As a formal deliberation council, the NWC confirmed the commitment to shared growth, an important political benefit. It also provided the government with a channel for learning from the enterprises about market realities and international competition. Cooperation between workers and employers meant that strikes were rare, thereby creating a pro-business environment conducive to investment and productivity enhancement.

The rule of law and protection of property rights

The *rule of law* is a key public good for governments to provide. Are contracts enforced in a low-cost manner? Are private property and an individual's personal security protected from predation by the more powerful? Under the rule of law, suits are settled through an effective and impartial judiciary on the basis of known laws, not through arbitrary dictates or discretionary authority as might be obtained with political connections. Also, no one is punishable except for a breach of law established in the ordinary courts. The rule of law effectively constrains the more powerful from opportunistically seizing private property. At the same time, it

14 Professor Lim Chong Yah was Chairman from 1972 to 2001, and in the words of Mauzy and Milne was "universally lauded for his contribution to building the tripartite mechanism." (Mauzy and Milne (2002), p. 207).

promotes welfare by enhancing cooperation among the citizenry. North considered the inability of governments to develop effective, low-cost enforcement of contracts as the main cause of under-development historically and today.[15] Singapore established a stable set of rules that protect contracts and property rights.

Law and order provides a framework for stability and development. Singapore believes in punishment including mandatory caning or death penalty for severe crimes as a more effective deterrent than long prison sentences. The number of executions, mainly for drug trafficking and murder, has come down to 12 a year on average in 2003–05. A recent survey found 85 percent of Singaporeans in favor of continued mandatory death sentencing for these crimes.[16] Caning for men between the ages of 16 and 50 is used as punishment, in addition to imprisonment, for crimes such as rape and robbery, as well as for some non-violent offenses such as vandalism. When Michael Fay, an 18-year old American, along with some Singaporean teenagers, was sentenced in 1994 to six strokes of the cane for going on a rampage and spray painting some 20 cars, the media and the government in America protested vigorously, although public opinion was reportedly divided.[17] Singapore is known for its strict law enforcement and stiff penalties for offenders. The World Economic Forum's competitiveness indicators accorded Singapore the highest rank for "full confidence among people that their person and property are protected."[18]

Upholding the principle of equality of all before the law at times requires ruthlessness and courage. In his memoirs, Lee Kuan Yew described how Singapore carried out the execution of three convicted Indonesians in 1968 despite threats of retaliation from Indonesia. Establishing the credibility and integrity of Singapore's financial system required firmness and consistency over many years. Singapore sought to prosecute a prominent British national for stock market

15 North (1990), p. 54.
16 Jeremy Au Yong, *Sunday Times*, February 12, 2006, News, p. 8.
17 Lee Kuan Yew (2000), p. 243.
18 World Economic Forum (2005).

manipulation in 1975 amid efforts by his government to protect him.[19] The MAS for several years resisted strong political pressure to lower its standards and grant a license to the National Bank of Brunei, a course of action vindicated when that bank was forced to close in 1986 following evidence of irregularities. The MAS also refused several times to award a license to the Bank of Commerce and Credit International (BCCI). That bank too went bankrupt in 1991 following improprieties that led to massive losses.

Establishing a first-rate judiciary took several years. In 1990, the judicial system was revamped to clear the congestion in the courts where some cases had been delayed for 4–6 years before coming to trial. Lee Kuan Yew stressed the importance of an objective and transparent mechanism for selecting the most capable and dedicated person as chief justice as well as adequate remuneration. In his memoirs, he describes how Yong Pang How, chief justice from 1990 until early 2006, provided leadership to the judges, selected the best ones on meritocratic principles, reformed the courts and their procedures, and introduced computerization. He reduced the backlog and delays by forcing amendments to the rules and practices that lawyers took advantage of to procrastinate and postpone their cases. He kept discipline in the courts, was systematic and fair, and understood the objectives of good government in a multiracial society.

By 1999, Singapore's court system had gained a high reputation for speed, efficiency, low cost, and fairness. Countries came to study it and the World Bank held it up as an example. International rating systems rank Singapore the highest in Asia, and globally ahead of the United States and the United Kingdom, for its fair administration of justice in society.[20] Singapore's success in this area, which has eluded so many countries, can be attributed to incentives that combine the carrot and the stick. The strategy involves selecting the best people,

19 Lee Kuan Yew (2000), Chapter 5.

20 For several years, the Hong Kong-based Political and Economic Risk Consultancy (PERC) ranked Singapore's judicial system as the best in Asia. The 2006 edition of the *Asia Pacific Legal 500*, a major legal guide in the region, states that, "Singapore's higher courts stand head and shoulders above those in neighboring countries."

and appealing to their sense of serving a noble cause and overcoming challenges as a team, while providing them attractive remuneration. The Chief Justice himself had already built his wealth in an earlier career as head of a successful commercial bank. Lawyers are disciplined for professional misconduct and subjected to strict timelines on litigation to ensure expeditious clearing of cases.

Steadfast and impartial application of the law helped Singapore's economy in many ways. It provided fundamental assurances to investors that their *property rights* were secure and that contracts would be enforced. It built confidence in the financial system. In addition, the low level of crime helped persuade MNCs to choose Singapore as their regional headquarters and an attractive place to relocate their employees and dependants. Singapore's constitution and various laws oblige respect and fair treatment for racial and religious minorities, which has contributed to social harmony. Adherence to the labor laws helped enforce constructive relations between labor and management. It strengthened the government and contributed to continuity of the policy and institutional environment.

Figures 4.1A and 4.1B illustrate the statistical association between the rule of law and the proximate causes of economic growth: factor accumulation and productivity gains.

In the figures, the rule of law is measured as a composite of: (i) the enforceability of contracts; (ii) the effectiveness and predictability of the judiciary; and (iii) the incidence of crime. Singapore ranks third among a group of 71 countries, preceded only by Switzerland and Austria, and ahead of Canada and the United States. In both cases, there is strong positive correlation, consistent with the expectation that where the rule of law is weak, factors of production would not be accumulated and economic activity would suffer from inefficiency.

Integrity of governance

Corruption is now widely regarded to be a major obstacle to economic and social development. It corrodes the institutional foundation on which growth depends. This need not imply that

Figure 4.1 The Rule of Law and Sources of Economic Growth[1]

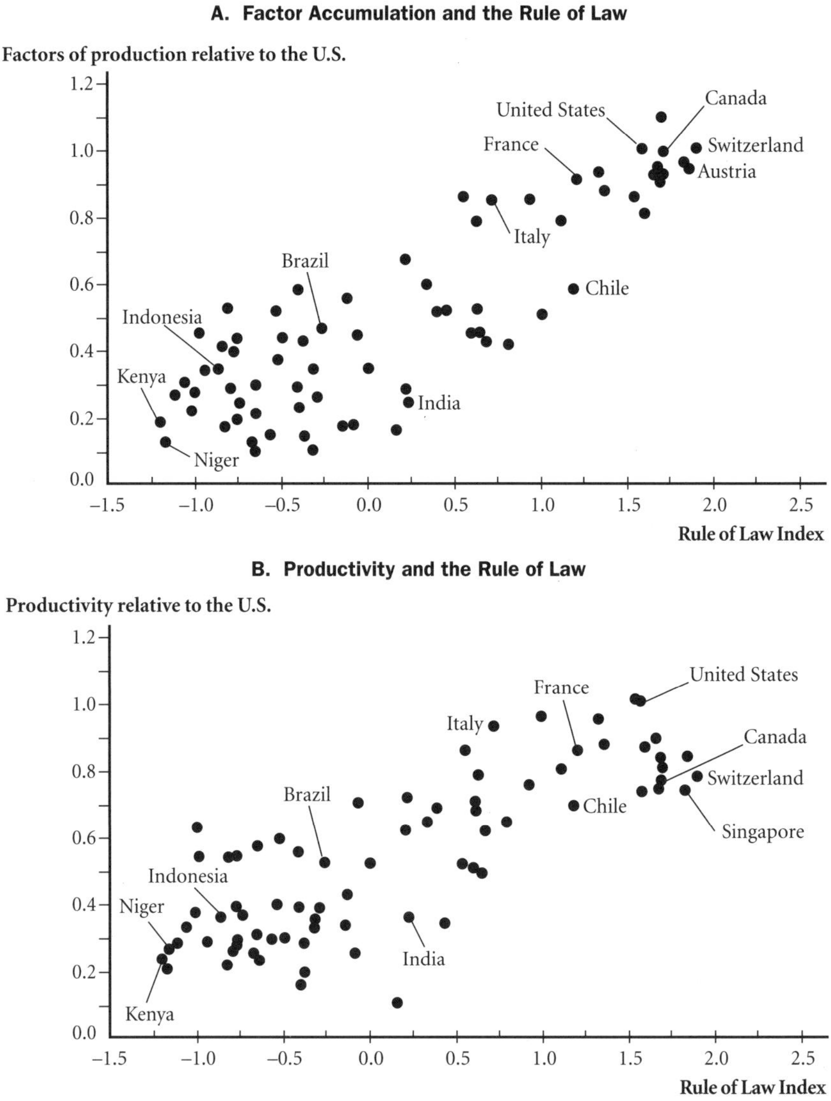

1 Data on the horizontal axes are from Kaufmann et al. (2002) for 71 countries, expressed in standard deviations and centered on zero. The vertical axes reflect a decomposition of output per worker in each country in1998, relative to the United States which is assigned a value of 1. For example, output per worker in India was 8.4 percent that of the United States. Physical and human capital per worker was 24 percent and TFP 35 percent of the levels prevailing in the United States. Both fractions multiplied corresponds to 0.084.

Source: Weil, D. (2005). *Economic Growth*, pp. 340–41 and pp. 186–190. © 2005 Pearson Education, Inc. Reprinted with permission.

economic growth is impossible in the presence of corruption: New York City in the 19th century, and Japan, South Korea, Taiwan, and China during more recent decades experienced robust growth without eradicating corruption.[21] Nonetheless, corruption, defined as the use of public power for private gain, is harmful in many ways. It requires higher taxes than would otherwise be needed or increases the fiscal deficit, encourages governments to design discretionary policies that create more opportunities for corruption, causes administrative processes to slow down to extract bribes for "speed money," and undermines the judiciary. It induces people to focus their energy and talents on the distribution of existing wealth and diverts from creating new wealth, which requires trust and access to opportunities. Corruption undermines the public's trust in legitimate regulation. It can be regarded as an arbitrary tax, often with a high degree of randomness that creates uncertainty and adds to the cost of establishing new businesses, particularly for small enterprises.[22]

Singapore boasts one the world's best ratings for low levels of corruption. A recent report of Transparency International ranks it fifth out of 159 countries, ahead of the United States and after Iceland, Finland, and New Zealand.[23] This was not always the case. Colonial Singapore had its share of petty corruption such as money tips to speed up customs inspections, and irregularities in government procurement, although probably less deeply embedded than in some other societies. With home rule in 1959, the government embarked on an anti-corruption strategy that over the decades has become highly effective. Its strategy minimized both incentives and opportunities for corruption. Key features are as follows:

First, *integrity of governance* started from the top. The anti-corruption campaign concentrated first on the big offenders at the higher levels. The government set high standards for itself, making

21 Weil (2005), Chapter 12.
22 Tanzi (1998).
23 Transparency International (2005).

sure that every dollar of expenditure was accounted for and reached its intended destination. No one, whether military or civilian, was above the law. On various occasions, the prime minister and several Cabinet members have defended themselves before the courts. World-renowned newspapers have been instructed by courts to withdraw insinuations or allegations of nepotism or corruption and have paid financial compensation to Singapore's leaders.

Second, the government insists on consistent prosecution of all transgressors, regardless of rank or position. Keeping high moral convictions required strong leadership. Anti-corruption officials must have full support from the top to enforce the rules. Attempts to bribe a civil servant are punishable by law. Civil servants found guilty of receiving bribes are not only prosecuted, but also lose their job and pension benefits and risk being denied reemployment in the private sector. Such deterrents contribute to high levels of probity. High-profile cases naturally make the headlines—Cabinet ministers have been convicted for soliciting or receiving bribes for aircraft purchases or land development. One minister in disgrace took his life.

Third, the deterrent of punishment is balanced by the reward of attractive levels of remuneration, on a par with comparable positions in the private sector. This is considered vital for high levels of probity in political leaders and high officials.[24] The high compensation of top ministers, civil servants, military, and judiciary—probably the highest in the world—is an area of contention in Singapore. It serves, however, not only to attract talent but also ward off temptations of using public office for private gain. As said by Lee Kuan Yew: "The high-minded approach that ministers are more than compensated by

24 "The formula sets salaries for ministers at two-thirds of the median income of 48 top private income earners from different professions such as bankers, engineers, lawyers...based on private sector income tax returns. The last publicly disclosed figures were for 2000, when the prime minister's annual salary was raised to S$1.94 million and that of the most junior minister was S$968,000." (*Straits Times*, July 1, 2000; quoted in Mauzy and Milne (2002), p. 61). The leadership has voluntarily forgone pay rises at times of economic difficulties such as in 2001 and 2003.

the power and honor of the office and that public service should entail a sacrifice of income is unrealistic. Underpaid ministers and public officials have ruined many governments in Asia."[25] Alternative solutions such as combining low official salaries with extensive semi-hidden perks or with subsequent lucrative contracts in the private sector were considered inferior. Adequate remuneration at lower levels also helps prevent corruption that is based more on need than greed. The system encourages politicians to put public service first and attends to their legitimate private interests.

Fourth, opportunities for corruption were minimized. In the economic sphere, Singapore's reliance on competitive market pricing has avoided the economic rents that come with lucrative monopolies, concessions, licenses, or import permits as were granted by President Marcos of the Philippines and President Suharto of Indonesia to relatives and associates. In the public service, discretion was reduced by specifying clear published guidelines and merit-based recruitment and promotion. Public servants in Singapore, and staff in private business as well, come across as being extremely rule-conscious. In the political sphere, Singapore has avoided a situation that is commonplace elsewhere, namely, where political parties and office holders have to expend large amounts of money to get elected, which once in office they wish to recuperate to prepare for the next election cycle. Short campaigning cycles and mandatory voting to reduce incentives for vote-buying are some of the methods used.

The Singapore government made integrity a top priority. Within a year of assuming office in 1959, a stringent—some will no doubt say draconian—anti-corruption law was enacted to replace a law established in colonial times. The 1960 law widened the definition of gratuity to anything of value, and gave investigators broad powers including arrest, search, and investigation of bank accounts of suspected persons and their wives, children, or agents. Proof that an accused was living beyond his or her means corroborated evidence of bribery. The law was further tightened in 1963, making

25 Lee Kuan Yew (2000), p. 196.

it compulsory for summoned witnesses to present themselves to give information.[26]

As explained by Lee Kuan Yew: "The PAP government set out to have a clean administration. We were sickened by the greed, corruption, and decadence of many Asian leaders...who let their societies slide backward." But so were the communists, the PAP's chief antagonists. "Disgust with the venality...of Nationalist Chinese leaders after the war made many young Singaporean students...in those days...admirers of the dedication and selflessness of the communists' revolutionary virtues and Spartan lives." Thus, the PAP's deep sense of mission led them to take the oath of office in June 1959 in white shirts and white pants "to symbolize the purity and honesty we stood for...That was what the people expected."[27] High moral principles, effective government, and political calculations coincided.

Social inclusion leading to political stability

Singapore aimed for social inclusion by finding cooperative solutions when people's preferences or choices differ. Memories of ethnic riots steered the young state resolutely in the direction of a multiracial, multi-ethnic, multi-religious tolerant society. There is high sensitivity to any rekindling of ethnic-religious tensions. Recently, the government was concerned about a potential backlash against Muslims should a terrorist attack be carried out by outside groups such as the Jemaah Islamiyah. National service is a rite of passage: a way of life that helps create unity among the different groups. Labor friction has been avoided through a combination of policies. An important factor has been improving economic opportunities, which reduces social polarization and frees energy for economic pursuits. When Malay students did poorly in science and mathematics relative to the other races, the government engaged community leaders to

---

26 Lee Kuan Yew (2000), Chapter 12.

27 Lee Kuan Yew, (2000), p. 183. The official all-white uniform of the PAP remains to this day.

help parents motivate their children to do better, and this produced results. Low inflation and rapid growth have contributed to social and political stability, a key factor for encouraging investment in fixed and human capital and for the productivity increases that pull resources to new sectors.

This concludes our discussion on institutions. Building institutions that are conducive to economic growth is a major challenge facing many governments. In Singapore, efficient public policy administration, adherence to the rule of law, high levels of integrity in governance, and social inclusion leading to political stability supported pro-growth economic policies. These formal and informal rules and norms determined opportunities and incentives faced by individuals and firms. Many societies waste vast resources in struggles to take possession of existing output or in other unproductive activities. In Singapore, institutions direct people's efforts toward the accumulation of physical and human capital and increased labor input, the acquisition and dissemination of new technologies, and the moving of capital and labor to sectors that produce high value.

CULTURAL ATTRIBUTES IN SUPPORT OF ECONOMIC GROWTH

So far, we have attributed Singapore's remarkable economic growth performance to the five proximate causes. We then analyzed how economic policies influenced these five sources of growth. Next, we examined how institutions allowed policies to be implemented—and directly influenced the five sources.

In this section, we take a look at culture—people's values, attitudes, and beliefs. Specifically, how did Singapore's cultural characteristics influence pro-growth policies and institutions, and in this way help shape the incentives and opportunities that fostered economic advance? Additionally, cultural features such as diligence, drive for excellence, openness to new ideas, trust, and ability to cooperate may have had a direct impact on the proximate sources.

However, in the absence of pro-growth policies and institutions cultural characteristics are unlikely to lead to fruition.[28]

"Culture" or "people's mindsets" is not frequently discussed in the economic development literature. By contrast, the role of "institutions" has become mainstream over the past 20 years. Institutions were not a new discovery. Gunnar Myrdal, Nobel Laureate for Economics in 1974, emphasized institutions as a key determinant of successful development in his monumental *Asian Drama* (1968). Myrdal went further, underlining the importance of attitudes and values in underpinning and interacting with institutions. He noted how attitudes prevailing in traditional, mainly rural, societies inhibited economic growth. A penetrating and candid mind, Myrdal attributed the reluctance of economists to discuss attitudes to a desire for political correctness. Intellectuals in the newly independent states, he observed, were sensitive to racial overtones and stereotyping, reminiscent of the pre-independence era when colonial powers pointed to anti-modernization attitudes among the locals to rationalize continuing backwardness.[29]

Reluctance to discuss culture has other reasons as well. Economists prefer areas that are more easily quantifiable. In addition, culture is difficult to observe in an unbiased manner: knowing that an economy has grown successfully, we may subconsciously look at the cultural features selectively.[30] Also, the direction of causality is ambiguous, because economic growth will alter a society's culture. Finally, economic growth itself, and its core underlying values, may leave us ambivalent. John Maynard Keynes, arguably the past century's best-known economist, considered the cultural attributes that promote economic growth—the love of money, the glorification of hard work,

28 Linking cultural attributes to institutions allows us to narrow but not bridge an ongoing debate. On one side are economists, who focus on incentives and opportunities as reflected in policies and institutions. The other side comprises sociologists in the tradition of Max Weber, who attributed 16th century growth in Northern Europe to the "Protestant ethic," and economic historians. Typical of the latter group is David Landes (1999), who stated that: "If we learn anything from the history of economic development, it is that culture makes all the difference."

29 Myrdal (1968), Prologue.

30 See Weil (2005), Chapter 14 on observer bias.

and the focus on how to improve things in the future rather than living in the moment—distasteful. Unfortunately, in his words: "Until the goal of economic growth has been achieved...avarice and precaution must be our gods for a little longer."[31]

Values were prominently discussed during the late 1980s and 1990s. The quest for explanations for the rapidly growing "East Asian miracle" economies drew attention to cultural features. Work ethic and thrift were common to Japan, Taiwan, South Korea, Hong Kong, and Singapore. These features embodied values that had been emphasized by Confucius some 2,500 years ago. The impressive results of these East Asian economies provided justifiable pride in many Asians, whom colonialism had conditioned to think of their societies as being inherently inferior. In Singapore, individualism and political liberalism were seen as inroads of Western culture and values. An "Asian values" debate ensued, which in its more unpalatable moments led to polarized polemics and defiance against the West for claiming superiority of the specifics of its own social and political institutions regardless of the sometimes very different conditions in which Asian societies found themselves. Many Asians, seeking a sense of self, dislike equating modernity, which they embrace, with Westernization. Kishore Mahbubani, Singapore's former ambassador to the United Nations, eloquently articulated these issues, which we will discuss in greater detail in Chapter 6.[32]

As to the descriptor of the values, some felt uncomfortable with the generalization of the term "Asian" for values that are associated with only part of the continent and that to a degree were quite prominent in 19th century Victorian England too.[33] The irony is that Asian values during colonial times were invoked to explain not the success but the lack of development of South Asia in particular. Asian

31 Keynes (1930).

32 Mahbubani (2002), in particular the essays "Can Asians think?" and "An Asian Perspective on Human Rights and Freedom of the Press."

33 Confucius celebrated the virtues of diligence and thrift some 2,500 years ago and John Calvin those of devotion to hard work and material success some 500 years ago.

values then referred to attitudes such as otherworldliness and spirituality that detracted from the drive for material progress. Jawaharlal Nehru, who became India's first prime minister, rejected this approach as being an undesired glorification of poverty.[34] Many would probably agree that the more successful socioeconomic systems and their future development blend elements of both Western and Eastern traditions.

Nonetheless, distinct cultural values, attitudes, and beliefs set Singapore apart from other, economically less successful societies. That is certainly the view of the government. Numerous government campaigns over the years sought to directly influence people's attitudes and behavior. Singaporeans have been instructed to abandon the old habit of spitting (which spreads tuberculosis), to take care of public property and newly planted trees in public areas, to stop littering (including of spent chewing gum on pavements), to maintain sanitary conditions in public toilets, and to be courteous to visitors and each other.[35] More fundamentally, the government continuously molds and reinforces values, considering them to be an integral element in implementing its policies and shape the country's institutions. Examples abound. To build a national army, the government deliberately set out to change the historical aversion of Singapore's Chinese majority to soldiering, which they regarded as low-grade employment. To ensure international competitiveness, the government intoned labor that remuneration must conform to work performed, not seniority. Values form the ideology of the PAP government and the set of beliefs that packages its institutions and policies. They also contribute to "branding" Singapore internationally and achieve national cohesion at home. Fundamental social and cultural changes have helped Singapore achieve its current success.

---

34 Myrdal (1968), p. 94.

35 Prime Minister Goh Chok Tong decided on the ban to import chewing gum in 1992 reportedly after vandals stuck gum on the sensors of the doors of the Mass Rapid Transit trains, causing the service to be disrupted. The ban was partially lifted in 2002.

Governments in other societies are less inclined to play such a role. Their population considers it paternalistic. The Singapore government has been ridiculed in the Western press for its tutelage as "PAP knows best" and creating a "nanny state." Elsewhere, churches, schools, and other parallel institutions fulfill that role. But the Singapore government wanted to educate its people to provide first-rate service, achieve First World standards in public and personal security, health, and transportation, and earn the brand name of "Southeast Asia's garden state." This was partly to earn the tourist dollar and enhance the city-state's attractiveness as a hub for the regional headquarters of MNCs, but no less importantly, to make life pleasing for all and to raise collective pride and self-esteem. In Lee Kuan Yew's words: "We wanted to become a civilized, cultivated society *in the shortest possible time* [author's emphasis]."[36] Western societies count more on bad habits disappearing on their own—over a longer period—but Singapore is rushed for time. It wants to catch up rapidly and to that end, organizes its society differently from the West.

What is the role of attitudes and values? In Singapore, what were the mindset and the culture that supported pro-growth institutions? Is there a body of beliefs that inform action and justify it? Without subscribing to the notion of Asian values, four themes can be distinguished as they have characterized Singapore over the past 40 years. A key issue is whether these values are inherent in Singapore as a society or have been inculcated by the PAP government. They certainly were strongly advocated by the government as part of its "socializing." But there also was receptivity with the populace and sufficient congruence for the values to have lent support to policies and institutions.

A long-term, forward-looking view

Singapore society is willing to take a long-term, forward-looking view. A high propensity to save—even after taking into account other

36 Lee Kuan Yew (2000), p. 211.

explanations such as evolving demographics or rising income—implies readiness to accept delayed gratification. Singaporeans heed the urging of their leaders to work hard, sacrifice now for enjoyment later, and to provide a better future for their children. Energetic enterprise and alertness to opportunities in a changing world are praised. The forward-looking view focuses on collective wealth creation over time, not redistribution of the existing pie. By contrast, societies that rapidly build up unfunded entitlement liabilities have a shorter time horizon and live more in the present. In the extreme, this leads to collective policy paralysis, rationalized by unrealistically optimistic assumptions about future conditions. Singapore's long-term macroeconomic assumptions are deliberately conservative.

Other societies find it difficult to focus wholeheartedly on the future. They may take a long-term view—backward. Groups in many countries find it extraordinarily difficult to overcome past collective traumas, ethnic, social, or religious; they cannot forget earlier injustices. The generations-old strife between Tamils and Sinhalese in Sri Lanka; the division of Kashmir that is rooted in earlier Muslim-Hindu antagonism between Pakistan and India; the difficult coexistence between descendants of the vanquished Incas, subsequently exploited in mines and excluded from national politics, and the Spanish conquerors in Bolivia, all breed instability. Even in Western Europe, lingering remnants of injustice among the social classes in the 19th century make it more difficult to galvanize society to take a constructive forward look. These historical traumas have used up much collective energy in other countries that the Singapore government recognized could be channeled toward forward-looking development, having resolutely opted for racial and religious harmony and multiculturalism and for "collective amnesia" of preexisting grievances.

Openness to new ideas and eagerness to learn imply a forward-looking view. David Landes describes how Europeans had great willingness to copy the best that other countries had to offer—in his view a key element of Europe's ascent. They readily adopted paper, gunpowder, and other inventions from the Chinese. Mid-19th century Japan, in turn, enthusiastically embraced ideas and technologies from Western Europe, even legal codes and institutions.[37] The Muslim world, by contrast, has generally been less open in recent decades. Singapore's leadership has eagerly learned from other countries, while adapting the findings to its own circumstances.[38]

Positive long-term, forward-looking views, with their promise of betterment, helped achieve social cohesion and political stability in Singapore. They encouraged the discipline of high private and public savings, and openness to new technology and more efficient processes. Holding up the benefits of collective wealth creation—over time—has helped suppress corruption and other unproductive activities that focus on the zero-sum game of short-term distribution. Long-term, forward-looking views of the people offer fertile soil for farsighted policies.

Working out mutually advantageous solutions through consensus

Trust is essential for the numerous transactions that make up a modern economy. Societies with a high degree of "social capital," that is, internal cohesion and willingness to help each other, tend to have higher rates of investment as well.[39] Emphasis on resolving issues through consensus rather than contention marks Singapore. Racial and religious harmony is seen as being vital for stability and is a

37 Landes (1999), Chapters 3 and 23.

38 Lee Kuan Yew (2000) mentions key ideas on early industrialization strategy derived from Dr Albert Winsemius and Professor Raymond Vernon. Israeli advisors gave valuable insight on military affairs and on setting up the EDB. Useful ideas were provided by J.P. Morgan bankers in 1992 on the need to prepare Singapore's banks for global competition and IT-based banking. New Zealand garden experts shared their knowledge on ways to keep Singapore green. Lee learned from Canada about phasing out smoking in public places, from Boston City how car certification could combat air pollution and how airport landing and take-off over the sea minimized noise pollution in urban zones; from Japan, quality control; and from Germany, technical education.

39 Weil (2005), p. 409.

critical ingredient for the tenor of Singapore society. Multiculturalism recognizes that people of various ethnicities have made Singapore their home and the tone is one of gentility and urbaneness. Singapore's constitution specifies four official languages. Malay, the language of a minority, became the national language. English, the principal education and working language, conferred a big advantage to Singapore as it became the lingua franca of the global economy.[40] Creating a climate of mutual confidence was important to persuading the MNCs to locate and stay in Singapore, to ensure constructive relations between labor and capital, and in Singapore's international relations. We review all three areas.

In his thorough historical analysis of Singapore, Carl Trocki (2005) noted how the PAP set aside its socialist ideology and entered a "strategic alliance with global capital." Indeed, Singapore welcomed the MNCs early on, not letting ideology stand in the way of rational reasoning. At the time, the neo-colonialist dependency school of thought led many developing countries to reject the MNCs. But the PAP felt that to stay in power, it had to create jobs for the many unemployed. Reliance on the MNCs allowed the PAP government to "leapfrog" over neighboring countries to the global economy and to circumvent local Chinese-educated entrepreneurs, who were not sympathetic to the PAP's agenda.

The government created a pro-business, market-driven environment. Anything the MNCs could reasonably wish for, Singapore provided. This included a non-belligerent and disciplined labor force that was willing to work at low wages initially and eager to build up skills thereafter. Singapore had few or no restrictions on currency movements, allowed unrestricted outward profit transfer, permitted 100 percent foreign ownership, and did not require minimal local sourcing. Tax exemptions were generous and profit tax rates were lowered over time. Companies obtained access to subsidized land and benefited from quality infrastructure provisions,

40 This contrasts with, for example, Bangladesh, which opted for Bengali as the language of instruction in public schools following the country's independence in 1971 through separation from West Pakistan.

including excellent air and seaport communication and land transport. They could trust that rules would not change arbitrarily to their disadvantage. Singapore provided political, economic, and financial stability, a sound currency, and continuity of policy. Personal security was assured and there was an overall friendly ambience. The government was efficient and honest. A large military budget and geopolitical understanding with the United States further reassured investors.

But the government made sure that what was good for MNCs was also good for Singaporeans. MNCs offered valuable market access, capital, and expertise. The industrial policy of subsidization was selective. Targeted industries that were regarded as desirable had to meet minimal criteria, first of employment and growth potential, later technical content and value-added, then willingness to bring R&D to Singapore. MNCs had to be able to export profitably from Singapore in sectors with strategic growth prospects, which required bringing over high-quality technology. They had to collaborate actively in training the local labor force to become skilled engineers and workers, able to compete globally with the best. MNCs provided Singapore access to best-practice technology embedded in imported capital goods and foreign expertise. Human capital, physical capital, and knowledge interacted. This was an effective way for Singapore to acquire knowledge. Countries with protected markets missed out on this type of learning.[41] MNCs were also expected to stay out of domestic politics, a requirement later generalized to "foreign talent" brought to Singapore for their expertise.

Trust went beyond assurances of access to a reliable court system and was more fundamental. Lee Kuan Yew relates how in the midst of the October 1973 oil embargo, the Singapore government decided to allow Shell, BP, Esso, and others to export their petroleum products that were stored in Singapore to any customers they wished wherever in the world. By putting long-term relationships ahead of short-term expediency and not insisting that Singapore be given

41 World Bank (1993).

priority delivery at the expense of other clients, goodwill was created, which later contributed to the decision of MNCs to expand their petrochemical operations in Singapore.[42] Symbiosis and partnership characterizes the relationship more than dependency. During the difficult years of 2001–03, the government eased costs for businesses, stressed the need for wage flexibility at times of adversity, and also lowered the profit tax rate.

Labor relations is a second area of building trust and consensus. The government had a deep commitment to a strategic vision that formed the foundation of labor relations. In Lee Kuan Yew's words: "The key to peace and harmony in society is a sense of fair play...that everyone has a share in the fruits of progress."[43] This required opportunity and reward to individuals and families to work harder, save more, study better. But to stay internationally competitive in labor-intensive exports, foreign investors wanted industrial peace: minimal strikes and a framework for orderly collective bargaining. To respond to that need, the government restrained independent unions and encouraged a cooperative climate in which labor was rewarded for increased productivity. For the workplace, this strategy envisaged partnership and cooperation to replace militancy and confrontation through legislation enacted in the late 1960s. As partner, labor received safeguards against abuse of power by employers, arbitration procedures through which the unions could protect the interests of their members, and legislation that encouraged maximum rewards for workers consistent with productivity. In turn, employers had their managerial prerogatives restored, allowing them to decide on recruitment, promotion, retrenchment, and work organization outside the framework of collective bargaining. This win-win arrangement led to high levels of investment and high returns on that investment, causing labor demand to soar.

42 Lee Kuan Yew (2000), p. 87.
43 Lee Kuan Yew (2000), p. 115.

A preference for cooperation and compromise over conflict marked Singapore's international relations as well. Although asserting the right to decide its own future, it negotiated, as best as it could, the timing and manner of the British withdrawal of their troops, which eventually took place in 1971, and supported Britain during the pound sterling crisis in the late 1960s by keeping Singapore's official reserves in that currency, thus seeking mutual benefit. While protecting its sovereignty in the years following independence, over time Singapore fostered greater regional economic interdependence. It was a founding member of ASEAN and continues to maintain the Association as a cornerstone of its foreign policy. In recent years, Singapore helped forge a broader Southeast Asian identity in light of the rise of India and China. Singapore seeks to maintain good relations with all major powers and to give each of them a stake in its progress and well-being. It brokered differences between China and Japan, and with both sides on the Taiwan issue. Quite remarkably, the government consistently presses a view on globalization that emphasizes the niches and opportunities that Singapore can find. It does so despite intense competition from lower-cost neighboring countries and rival economies, some with deep pockets, who also embrace similar strategies of economic growth, be they based on tourism or knowledge- and innovation-intensive sectors. Competition, while not exactly welcomed, is nonetheless praised as a positive-sum game.

Self-reliance and solidarity within the narrow family

After World War II, the industrial countries developed elaborate welfare states that provided national healthcare, generous unemployment insurance, and old-age pensions. The resulting income transfers responded to broadly held notions of equity and have contributed to social stability, but at a cost. Intergenerational transfers have resulted in unfunded future liabilities. Also, distorted incentives have enhanced individuals' dependence on the state, burdened government budgets, and lowered economic growth. Only a few countries, mainly in Northern Europe, appear to have succeeded in combining extensive state-sponsored social solidarity with strong global competitiveness.

In Singapore, the government makes only very limited social transfer payments for old-age, unemployment, the poor, and the sick. It emphasizes self-reliance through individual savings and purchased insurance. When these are insufficient, solidarity within the family becomes key, with the state available only as a last resort. The CPF and income tax system have institutionalized these provisions. Filial devotion toward one's parents and immediate relatives is strong. In fact, this virtuous attribute has been sanctioned into a legal obligation when children have the financial means.[44]

The financial self-reliance of the narrow family in Singapore also contrasts with the traditional extended family that one finds in countries such as the Philippines. Sharing within the extended family may have been essential for human survival in hunter-gatherer societies. However, when distant relatives feel entitled to their share from individuals who innovate, work hard, and progress financially, the solidarity discourages work and innovation.

In Singapore, the narrow family, although the center of solidarity, is also the seat of private property. The PAP government responded to a deep sense of private property, fundamentally a bourgeois value. The government felt that Singaporeans would protect their home and other property they owned and that personal savings would enhance their self-esteem and sense of responsibility.

Undoubtedly, the government promoted the values of self-reliance, family solidarity, and private ownership very actively in support of its economic policies. Whether ties within the narrow family will stay that strong with changing lifestyles that focus increasingly on the even smaller nuclear family, remains to be seen. For the past four decades, however, emphasis on these values has

---

44 The "Maintenance of Parents Act" came into force in 1995 to give parents above age 60 who could not support themselves, the legal means to claim maintenance from their children.

supported economic growth in Singapore. Self-reliance combined with a long-term vision have led to the pursuit of excellence, part of Singapore's trademark, along with stability.

Willingness to accept authority and paternalistic rule

Singaporeans heed the urging of their government to subordinate personal interest, not only to family but also to the society at large. Individuals are more willing to put community above their personal right to dissent than is the case in other countries. Respect for elders and agreeing with superiors is deemed important to help preserve "face." Hierarchy and authority are less challenged and ridiculing leaders is not done. Paternalistic rule is not as resented as might be expected. This also holds for the workplace where top-down approaches dominate and open disagreement and debate are less common than elsewhere. A sense of patriotism and sacrifice has made possible substantial cost-cutting during recessionary periods. The populace accepts that public funds in education are allocated with economic growth in mind: access is based on merit and curriculum offerings are determined by functional usefulness to society, not an individual's personal interests. Two years of mandatory military conscription for men, and for the majority Chinese the tradition of a hierarchical culture may have made it easier to rally people behind the leadership.[45]

Among a significant minority of Singaporeans, there is a yearning for a more contested democracy and greater political openness.[46] Some younger ones in particular may find the atmosphere too stifling and vote with their feet by emigrating. Also, there are limits to public acceptance of paternalism and requirement to conform. Two examples come to mind. In 1983, the government bemoaned the observed tendency of male university graduates to marry less-educated women and urged them to marry their equals, defined by

45 National service lasted 30 months for officers until 2004.
46 Mauzy and Milne (2002), p. 197. See also Chee (2001) and George (2000).

educational class—an admonition which not everyone appreciated.[47] On a related subject, when the 1980 census revealed that many women with university degrees were single and that those who did marry had fewer children than less-educated women, the government responded. It introduced the Graduate Mothers Scheme in June 1984, which provided direct financial and other benefits to women who had a third child, but only if they had a university degree. The scheme proved unpopular, including among some Cabinet ministers, and was withdrawn 12 months later to be subsequently revised.

Nonetheless, there seems to be an unwritten pact between the government and the population at large. As one observer summed it up: "The PAP government delivered employment and unprecedented prosperity, distributed among the population in a reasonably equitable manner, including the provision of education and public goods such as social stability and freedom from ordinary crime. In return, the Singaporean populace was willing to accept discipline, compliant labor relations, less personal liberty and self-expression, and more limited political openness, and to give one political party many times a renewed license to implement its long-term strategic vision. A majority of Singaporeans seems to have accepted this trade-off. Not everyone might find this an inspiring bargain but it has worked in Singapore."[48]

Willingness to take a long-term, forward-looking view; openness to cooperative win-win situations based on trust; self-reliance and solidarity within the narrow family; and acceptance of authority and benevolent paternalistic rule are cultural attributes that helped define the Singapore ethos. They correspond to the experiences, traditions, and expectations of the people. But the government further imbued them to shape the nation's character and buttress Singapore's strong pro-growth institutions and policies.

---

47 Lee Kuan Yew himself married Miss Kwa Geok Choo, the one girl in the class who beat him in English and economics. Lee (1998), Chapter 1.

48 Huff (1999), p. 44.

Five Improving Institutions: The Political Economy of Implementation

Gaining support for judicious policies and growth-enhancing institutions proves extraordinarily difficult in many countries. Numerous developing countries face daunting difficulty in building an honest and efficient government and civil service or in creating the conditions for political and social stability. Many advanced countries find it hard to implement the measures needed to place the finances for their aging populations on a sound footing, or to integrate into their societies the immigrants that their economies need in order to maintain their workforces. Singapore inherited some institutional advantages when the PAP government assumed power in 1959. But major institutional transformation occurred during the subsequent 45 years. Why and how did Singapore succeed in forging a consensus for building the social and political institutions in support of long-term policies for economic development?

Powerful forces tend to maintain existing institutions in all societies. Institutions are steeped in history. They have been chosen through social conflict for their distribution of income, rents, and privileges by groups with the political power to impose their own preferences. Yet major institutional change does occur. Sometimes, the change has been abrupt, as with the Meiji Restoration in Japan in 1867–68, China's market-oriented reforms after Mao Zedong's death in 1976, and the demise of the Soviet Union after the fall of the Berlin Wall in 1989. In other countries, institutional transformation was spread out over a longer period.

Elites, as pointed out by Daran Acemoglu, widen access to economic opportunities when they find it in their interest to do so.[1]

1 Acemoglu et al. (2004).

In some situations, as prevailed in Western Europe over the past century and a half, non-elite groups increasingly challenge the existing distribution of privileges. They fight for access, which the elite grudgingly concedes, in order to protect its own survival. The other situation occurs when the elites themselves realize that the old order has exhausted itself. They conclude that widening access is the best way for them to preserve their privileges and influence and to realize their own potential and that of their offspring.

Singapore's experience falls under the second category. Carl Trocki describes how the English-educated Chinese professional class, which dominated the moderate wing of the PAP, rose to power.[2] Often, their fathers and grandfathers belonged to the Chinese Baba merchant class. During the colonial period, this class had allied themselves with Western traders under the protection of British rule. Lee Kuan Yew's family belonged to this upper-middle class. His father worked for Shell and one grandfather was an avowed Anglophile. Singapore's subsequent choice of an economic growth strategy, which was centered on partnership with MNCs, fits in quite naturally with this background. Several among these younger elite returned to Singapore in the 1950s with degrees earned from top English universities. There they had firmed their resolve to strive for independence from British rule. The rival group in Singapore comprised Chinese-educated businessmen, students, and laborers, many heavily communist-inspired who found their voice with the radical wing of the PAP.

The pursuit of political power, ultimately out of collective self-interest and possibly subconsciously, need not preclude idealistic leadership. In Singapore, both went together. The Japanese Occupation in 1942–45 had traumatized the populace. After the war, the young elite resented the domination and cruelty inflicted upon the locals. British rule had not protected Singaporeans. Personal survival had been at stake. Only through sheer cunning and alertness did Lee Kuan Yew escape a mass execution of thousands of young

2 Trocki (2005).

Chinese men at the hands of the Japanese.[3] Self-respect drove the young elite to strive for independence. As Lee Kuan Yew put it: "We may have been bourgeois English-educated leaders, but we stood up for the people who had given us a mandate in 1959." Singapore's early leaders had abiding political convictions that went back to their student days in England. The difficult struggles of the early decades resulted in strong bonds. They had a deep commitment to Singapore's future and felt responsible for its people.[4] Years later, in 1993, Lee reminisces: "...fish returned to the Singapore River...Clean rivers made possible a different quality of life...People sunbathed on the banks...For those who remember the Singapore River when it was a sewer, it is a dream to walk along its banks."[5] Such can be the pleasure of power, leading the pack safely to a better land.

In 12 years' time, by 1971, the moderate PAP government had fully consolidated its power and put in place its overall strategy. Its dominance over competing interest groups allowed consistent implementation of a coherent set of long-term development policies. Many other countries have had concentrated power, although nowhere near the development success of Singapore.

THE STRATEGY OF THE ELITE

"There is little doubt that the PAP leaders are elitist," wrote Mauzy and Milne. "They admire the power of the intellect, and they believe that only a few of the best and brightest are capable of leading well."[6] The elite, in the Singapore context, however, is merit based. Unlike in some other countries, it is not a closed, privileged, hereditary social class that succeeded in capturing the state. The strategy that the governing elite selected was conducive to political implementation of growth-enhancing institutions. Three features can be identified that many other countries lacked.

3 Lee Kuan Yew (1998), p. 56.
4 Lee Kuan Yew (2000), p. 226.
5 Lee Kuan Yew (2000), p. 207.
6 Mauzy and Milne (2002), p. 53.

First, a long-term vision of economic growth became Singapore's central focus. Other goals coexisted, such as survival as an independent country, building a national identity, and ultimately reaching First World standards in the arts and culture. But economic growth was needed to help fulfill these other national goals. The primacy of achieving long-term economic prosperity for society as a whole set Singapore apart from many other nations. Goh Keng Swee, Singapore's first finance minister and also defense minister, expressed it succinctly: "We must strive continuously to achieve economic growth, which requires political stability, and should not be distracted by other goals."[7] Other goals were thus subordinated, such as ideological notions of achieving redistributive justice via social transfers or tax policy. Communist countries had different priorities. China's primary preoccupation, until 1976, was to wrest power for the peasant class by breaking a four-millennium-old feudal order, and to rebuild the nation.[8] Only in 1982 did Deng Xiaoping declare as a primary goal turning China into a modern prosperous country by reforming and opening up its economy. Still other countries channeled vast collective energy into restoring an earlier balance of political or economic power between different ethnic, racial, or religious groups. Or they went to war over border disputes, often resulting in negative productivity growth, meaning that total output declined even if inputs increased. Pervasive uncertainty precluded high levels of investment and talented individuals emigrated or perished.

Singapore's elite had none of that: "Unless you have economic growth, you die"[9] was the government's maxim. Divisiveness was shunned. Singapore, as consecrated in its constitution, is a multiracial society that accords equality to all citizens regardless of race, language, or religion. Laws enforce this. There is constant concern not to upset internal balances and to maintain stability.

7 Goh Keng Swee (1976), p. 165.
8 Mahbubani K. (2002), p. 117.
9 Chew, M. (1996), p. 149.

Engineering prosperity for all was the best way to preserve internal cohesion, ethnic peace, and harmony, and to survive. Economic growth became the beacon for the city-state's collective destiny, not just to survive, but to prevail through superior performance.

Second, in Singapore, the governing elite chose a strategy that would share the benefits of economic growth among the populace—not through income redistribution policies, which tend to impede economic growth. Instead, the preferred strategy was to arm men and women with the means and opportunities to earn a living and acquire assets for their families by raising the skill level, including of lower income groups, and thus ensure upward mobility. For Singapore's elite, this win-win offer was perfectly rational: wealth would be shared or it would not exist. The only viable model was export-led growth that would take advantage of Singapore's location and make optimal use of its one resource, its people, creating social unity in the process. The dearth of landed estates and other natural resources precluded the feudal model as a source of privileges. However noble the intentions underlying Singapore's social policies, it was in the elite's own interest to more widely extend economic opportunities, such as education, and thereby expand its own group to new entrants. Universal education and numerous scholarships helped bright children of poor parents make it through university. This contrasts with the elite groups in some other countries. Feudal aristocracies in countries such as Pakistan with extensive landed property were willing to broaden their circle to include industrialists under import-substitution policies.[10] They would not, however, provide quality education on a large scale to girls and boys in rural areas, lest their power slip away. The result in many instances has been a low-level equilibrium with poor agricultural yields, harking back to an older model of apportioning economic rents, not creating new wealth.

Third, the politically dominant group in Singapore was willing to be held accountable. Although political participation is constrained

---

10 Husain (1999).

in Singapore, it needs emphasizing that the elite freely accepted limits on the exercise of power by the government. It accepted checks and balances that curb the natural tendency of power to corrupt. This set Singapore apart from dictatorships, kleptocracies, and regimes under arbitrary personal rule and helped legitimize the government. Several aspects can be highlighted. Firstly, Singapore's judiciary acts as a check on political power. Top government officials are accountable before the courts, and have been summoned. Lee Kuan Yew and his son, Lee Hsien Loong, both underwent a thorough court investigation in 1996 for allegations of real-estate improprieties and were acquitted. International surveys routinely rank the city-state very high for maintaining the rule of law, upholding property rights, and using the law to maintain probity of politicians and civil servants. Secondly, the dominant party regime does not imply absence of democracy: parliamentary elections are held within a five-year term limit, most recently in May 2006. Elections are contested freely. There is no ballot rigging or intimidation of voters. Singaporeans have the means to change their government democratically, although major obstacles are placed in the way of the opposition."[11] The PAP's dominance over the opposition parties since the late 1960s, its advantage of incumbency, and the electoral rules it has crafted over the years gave the party commanding heights: often victory was assured before Election Day due to a dearth of opposition candidates. Nonetheless, voting outcome, which has ranged from 61 percent in favor of the PAP in 1991 to 75 percent in 2001, and was 67 percent in May 2006, serves as a scorecard of popular approval. As felt by the government, the periodic requirement to seek a renewed mandate in

11 Opposition parties are constrained on donations they can receive and in the manner they can make their views known to the electorate. The PAP uses the advantage of incumbency. Prior to elections, which the government can time, the budget "redistributes" some accumulated budgetary savings back to the people, in the form of equity share distributions, "topping-up" of various CPF accounts, and for the poorer ones, rebates for utilities or house rental. The PAP also openly warns the citizenry that constituencies who vote for the opposition will be last in line to receive budgetary outlays for improving their housing estates, a significant financial drawback.

front of the electorate is a powerful spur to deliver the shared prosperity, personal safety, and public order, which voters have come to expect.[12] By creating widespread employment opportunities and improving living conditions, the politically dominant group in Singapore acquired and kept a popular mandate to pursue its long-term economic growth strategy. Thirdly, another countervailing force in Singapore's case, somewhat unusual but influential nonetheless in the current highly competitive globalized environment, is the MNCs. Singapore's strategic dependence on the MNCs as an engine of economic growth provided an additional check against some types of government failure, since political stability, a non-corrupt government, and sound economic management are critical to boosting investor confidence in the Singapore economy. Singapore combines a strong state with atomistic markets, rather than a strong state with monopolistic market power.

In sum, Singapore's elite, which established power in the 1960s, subsequently co-opted talent from across society and succeeded in building growth-enhancing institutions. It succeeded by choosing as the central priority a strategy of long-term economic growth. It widely shared the opportunities to participate in that growth and was prepared to be held accountable for its exercise of power. All three features set Singapore apart from many other countries. The dominant group in society established an accepted social contract for a viable long-term strategy.

That strategy was in the best interest of the elite—and the people. The PAP realized that it had to improve economic conditions to prevent the communists from focusing on the grievances of the unemployed. Singapore lacked natural resources to divide as spoils. Once political power was consolidated there were no rival groups to be placated through bribery. In fact, a high level of integrity strengthened the PAP's power. This insightful strategy enabled the

12 Lee Kuan Yew (2000) on why he had to be demanding of his ministers. Note also his statement: "Neglecting the working class or 'native' areas and planting greenery and cleaning up only where the rich live would have been politically disastrous for an elected government," p. 202.

elite not just to survive but to thrive at the head of a secure, respected, and dynamic nation. Self-actualization was achieved by helping the citizenry attain its full potential. This was a powerful incentive and the elite seized the opportunity. The coincidence of self-interest of the elite and development of the people was fortuitous and a cornerstone of Singapore's success.

GOVERNMENT TACTICS FOR INSTITUTION BUILDING

No comprehensive handbook is available, to my knowledge, which would readily guide governments in the political economy of implementing strategies for building pro-growth institutions. Communist parties, by contrast, used to develop how-to manuals on tactical steps for wresting power and achieving their goals: a standard example was infiltrating nationalist independence movements and once inside, turning them to the communist cause. Several ideas on tactics are available, however. The World Bank shares some conclusions from its work with countries on how to improve public sector governance.[13] What practical steps did the Singapore government take to implement its ambitious long-term strategy? In the following sections, three themes are developed.

Earning and keeping the people's trust

Singapore's government earned the people's trust by *building a record of economic success*. It consolidated its power by ensuring the credibility of promises made. Targets set were realistic—and were achieved or surpassed. By 1972, unemployment was conquered. Large undertakings were broken up into smaller, more manageable tasks, facilitated by having a long-term vision. Reforms were introduced sequentially, not all at once. Many of the more demanding ones, such as judicial and tax administration reforms, were implemented only in recent decades, in line with evolving views

13 World Bank (2005b), Chapter 9.

internationally on their importance. The government delivered on its promises to offer tangible benefits. Housing, education, and training underpinned economic growth and raised living standards. Economic plans were carefully engineered to help ensure their success. Success breeds success, and this built confidence, locally and from foreign investors. The PAP justified its uninterrupted rule by producing results.

The government kept the large majority of the population on its side. It had a good feedback system on policies with the community. When reforms were unavoidable, it spelled out the rationale. This was not easy. In the words of Lee Kuan Yew: "Every resettlement of hawkers, pig farms, or cottage industrialists involved haggling. They were never happy to move. This was a hazardous political task…It required empathy and delicate handling…or it would cost us votes in the next election…Even then, painful decisions had to be taken—in the interest of the majority. Older farmers who were resettled from their rural homesteads into high-rise flats missed their chickens, ducks, and vegetable plots. They voted against the PAP, even 20 years later. They felt the government had destroyed their way of life."[14] In the end, rationality prevailed. Their pain was many children's gain.

The government made diligent efforts to market and explain the rationale for its policies, particularly the unpopular ones. The government may be elitist in the sense of meritocratic but it is not aloof. Policies were not dictated. Individual union leaders were won over in the late 1960s through diligent, patient, and respectful explaining in face-to-face sessions by key government officials with outstanding communication skills.[15] Careful political management preceded the introduction in 1994 of the Goods and Services Tax (GST), a value-added type consumer tax.[16] The government prepared the people for the introduction of the Electronic Road Pricing (ERP) in 1999. In 1998, Lee Hsien Loong, then deputy prime minister, had to manage the politically difficult issue of lowering the employers'

14 Lee Kuan Yew (2000), p. 207.
15 Lee Kuan Yew (2000), p. 105.
16 Asher (2002), p. 414.

contribution to the CPF. Proposals were not produced with a flourish out of a hat. They were gradually unveiled as a hypothetical last-resort policy, which through public dialogue about the various alternatives became increasingly perceived as inevitable.[17] In the government's view, if there is a need to change policy, it is important to prepare the people early and explain why the change is necessary.

The government spent political capital sparingly, avoiding reforms that would backfire. It did not always succeed, however. Its foray into population engineering was such an exception, and it cost them some votes.[18]

Channeling collective emotions toward economic growth

Singapore's leaders invoked threats to the country's physical survival to spur economic performance. The threats were real. The brutal Japanese Occupation in 1942–45 made it clear to all that survival could not be taken for granted. After the war, communism became a menace to the region. As a successful, predominantly Chinese state that is but a speck in a Malay region, Singapore felt insecure. Sukarno's hostility over Singapore's participation in the Malaysian Federation and the bloodbath in Indonesia in October 1965 when General Suharto put down a coup by pro-communist officers caused trepidation. The fanaticism that had incited racial riots in Singapore in 1964 and lingered on threatened the lives of Lee and his family in 1965. Periodic friction with Malaysia, including threats to cut off the vital supply of potable water that Malaysia sells to Singapore, drove Singaporeans to band together. Failure to prevail, their government told them, would mean reabsorption into Malaysia and become another state like Penang or Malacca. As one observer put it: "A sense

17 Mauzy and Milne (2002), p. 123.

18 Lee Kuan Yew's views on the unequal distribution of talent in society and possible implications for the desirability of procreation by different groups are most controversial. Lee has responded that he was "not interested in being politically correct...but in being correct." (*Fortune*, July 21, 1997, pp. 31 and 36).

of siege and culture of insecurity...underlies Singapore's obsession with vigilance."[19] Risks of terrorist acts have added to uncertainty.

Rather than provoking enmity, the feeling of being under threat from abroad and also at home was internalized into a positive force. Singapore defended its sovereignty through establishing effective armed forces, and defense became part of its value system. The importance of racial harmony, and thus compromise, for survival is constantly held up. Memories of earlier traumas have been evoked frequently and have been used to help build internal cohesion within the nation. This is not unlike Western Europe, where the tragedy of two world wars—in this case between nations—generated goodwill among ex-combatants to compromise within the EU framework. Fear of crisis and internal and external enemies was invoked to energize the people, to make Singapore rugged and resilient, and to close ranks with the PAP, thus legitimizing the trustee role of the PAP in leading the pack safely through danger.

As physical threats to the young nation receded, economic survival came to the fore. Vulnerability of the economy to outside forces is not in doubt. Economic collapse was feared when the British announced in 1967 their intention to close their military bases before end-1971. Estimates of the prospective annual economic loss went as high as one-fifth of GDP. The government used the deep sense of crisis at the prospect of the British departure to demonstrate the disastrous consequences of strikes for the workers' self-interest. The fear galvanized the young nation to build social consensus for labor-intensive, export-led industrialization. Singapore showed no rancor, no blaming of outsiders. It did not ask for foreign aid—although the situation was difficult. Yet, by 1971, the transformation had been completed and labor had found new jobs, thanks to investments.

More economic shocks followed. The oil crises of the 1970s, the decline in global demand that caused economic recessions in 1985 and 2001, the Asian financial crisis in 1997, and the SARS epidemic

19 Leifer (2000), p. 4.

of 2003 that sharply cut travel to Singapore, all severely shocked the economy. In each case, what stood out was the way in which the country responded. Each crisis was seen as the spur Singapore needed for a new round of restructuring, diversification, and innovation—in line with Arnold Toynbee's view of history as challenge and response.

Intensifying global competition is seen as providing both challenge and opportunity. Innovative responses fashioned by Singapore risk being copied elsewhere. Singapore must move fast to keep up with economic rivals. Comparative advantages were eroded by low-cost competition. But rather than lament the consequences, Singapore's leaders emphasized new opportunities. A recent public address by Senior Minister Goh Chok Tong is typical. Celebrating the 15th anniversary of Nanyang Technological University, he stressed the need for constant reinvention, citing the Darwinian dictum that "even the strong perish unless they adapt."[20]

Beyond survival, catching up economically with the West has been another rallying cry for Singapore. Specific targets are set and updated periodically, for example to reach the per capita income level of the United States by 2030 or the Netherlands by 2020 as was specified in the Strategic Plan of 1991.[21] Investment in technological infrastructure and continual upgrading of innovation capabilities is urged, to help reduce the technological gap with advanced economies and become a high-income economy.

To catch up, Singaporeans urge each other, and drive themselves, to excel. The trait of unforgiving self-perfection is humorously referred to by Singaporeans as "kiasu," Hokkien for "afraid to lose" or "afraid to lose out and not get one's share." For the economy, there is constant preoccupation with developing new niches of excellence, most recently in integrated tourist resorts, digital movie studios, and advanced water treatment technology.

---

20 Quoted in the *Straits Times*, December 18, 2005.
21 Ministry of Trade and Industry (1991).

Tactics to acquire and consolidate power

Turning the strategic vision of shared prosperity into reality required highly determined and skilful political leadership. To deliver its side of the social contract, the government employed a range of tactics and sequenced them for optimal effect as events unfolded in order to acquire and consolidate power. It used this power to ensure implementation of its program of economic policies and institution building.

Singapore's leadership was industrious and intelligent in practical ways. Like parties in power elsewhere, it uses budgetary and other advantages of incumbency prior to elections. Tactical mistakes by adversaries were shrewdly exploited early on. Under Lee Kuan Yew, the moderate wing of the PAP outmaneuvered its opponents. On the eve of the 1961 election, the more extreme PAP members and pro-Communist trade union leaders formed a new radical party: the Barisan Socialis. Their main platform was immediate full independence from Britain and early departure of the British military. Lee rightly realized that voters would instead be swayed by a credible promise of job creation and better living conditions through economic expansion. The PAP has proclaimed the superiority of its strategy ever since: "No one will deliver the economic goods better." Two years later, a shrewd sense of timing led Lee Kuan Yew to exploit a temporary weakness of the Barisan. He called a surprise election on September 22, 1963, just six days after Singapore had joined the Malaysian Federation, over the Barisan's objection, and won by a landslide.

The PAP was ruthless when they considered it necessary. Immediately following the 1963 election victory, the government arrested and detained 15 prominent leaders of the opposition on the grounds that they were preparing a communist plot. This crippled the opposition. Already in 1959, Albert Winsemius had warned Lee Kuan Yew that eliminating the communists as a force would be vital in winning over the unions in favor of an economic strategy that required their constructive cooperation. The PAP's bold action against the Barisan Socialis had neutralized the communist opposition, and with them the extreme left-wing union members. Harsh confrontation with recalcitrant union leaders still occurred and was not avoided in 1968, leading to delisting of their union after they had called an illegal strike, although workers who cooperated kept their jobs. The PAP has proved to be a formidable and fiercely competitive opponent, ever since. The lack of a credible opposition has been attributed to the authoritarian ways of the PAP. For example, it has periodically invoked the Internal Security Act (ISA) to round up "communists and communalists" and detain them without trial, in one case for 23 years. There are no reports of political prisoners any longer.[22] After the 1997 elections, PAP leaders mounted numerous successful defamation suits against one opposition party member for inflammatory remarks that he had made. The legal defense costs of the suits drove him into bankruptcy, which by law made him ineligible to stay in Parliament.

Terrain once conquered was secured through formal legislation. It would then be defended through the rule of law. Existing legislation was systematically used or strengthened, and new legislation enacted, both to consolidate power and to underpin the development strategy. The anti-subversion legislation, introduced by the British in 1948 that sanctioned arrest and detention without trial was kept on the books. To this day, the authorities have sweeping powers, including for control of public protest. Electoral rules further consolidated political power in favor of the PAP.[23] Laws have been enacted that constrain ownership and freedom of action of the press and there is strong legal protection against slander. In Lee Kuan Yew's

22 United States Government, Department of State (2006).

23 Most members of Parliament are elected from Group Representation Constituencies (GRCs), which were introduced for the 1988 general election. GRCs require parties to put forward a team of 3–6 members, including at least one member of an ethnic minority group. The party with a plurality wins all the seats. Critics denounce the innovation as a conspiracy to weaken the opposition. They contend that a strong candidate from an opposition party may fail to be elected because of the weakness of team mates. By contrast, a PAP candidate with weak electoral appeal can be elected if he or she is part of a GRC led by a popular minister.

words: "First, we educated and exhorted our people...After we had persuaded and won over a majority, we *legislated* [author's emphasis] to punish the willful minority."[24]

Legislation underpinned and consolidated the economic strategy. The constitution was carefully drafted to establish balance between the ethnic groups, with explicit provisions to create a tolerant multiracial society. Legislation enacted in 1968 anchored the trade union movement into the government's economic strategy.[25] Fiscal conservatism, once in place, was codified. In Singapore, by law, the budget must be balanced or in surplus over the tenure of a government. Budgetary savings accumulated before the beginning of a government's tenure, cannot be touched except with authorization of the president. By law, only individuals screened to have "high moral character" and meet other stringent tests, such as having extensive executive and financial experience, are eligible to stand for presidential election. In Singapore, practice preceded rules. Sometimes, countries are persuaded to vote into law or accept a rule that will tie their hands and by force of law or prior commitment, oblige them to engage in desirable economic policies. Fiscal rules governing budgetary policy in member-countries of the Euro-zone come to mind, or a currency board arrangement such as in Argentina in the 1990s, with pre-specified penalties for breaking the self-imposed rules. While fiscal responsibility laws can improve transparency and predictability, by themselves they cannot buy policy credibility. In Singapore's case, society supported fiscal rectitude. Legislation provided an additional safety latch to secure a door that was already locked through actual practice backed by power and conviction.[26]

---

24 Lee Kuan Yew (2000), p. 211.

25 Legislation enacted in 1967 banned strikes and lockouts in public utilities in order to protect the public interest. The Employment Act of 1968 enshrined in legislation the principle that wage negotiations should be based on economic growth and efficiency, rather than on abstract notions of justice. The Industrial Relations (Amendment) Bill of 1968 reversed union practices that had usurped employer prerogatives. It was instrumental in attracting substantial investment and creating new employment.

26 The Board of Commissioners of Currency, Singapore (BCCS) was established in 1967. Although not strictly a currency board system, it did provide institutional confidence for monetary policy.

The PAP leadership gained cooperation and cultivated allies. Some alliances were opportunistic and would shift with time as circumstances changed. These included the cooperation with the radical left in the 1950s, with the right wing Malaysian Prime Minister Tunku Abdul Rahman against the Barisan Socialis, and with the British in the 1960s to gain their support for Singapore's entry to the Malaysian Federation. Other relationships, with labor unions in particular, were long-standing and more firmly based on principle. The government associated, and even integrated, the unions as much as possible with its policies. The PAP used the National Trades Union Congress (NTUC), the labor umbrella organization, to discipline and socialize workers to the values of hard work and loyalty. In 1982, the Trade Unions (Amendment) Act defined the function of unions as promoting good industrial relations between employees and employers and to raise productivity for the mutual benefit of all involved. The PAP also encouraged unions to organize workers into production cooperatives such as supermarkets and taxi service to give them a stake in the economy. Over time, a symbiotic relationship developed between the PAP government and the NTUC that has been a central nexus in Singapore's economic success. For many years the secretary-general of the NTUC has also been a Cabinet minister in the government. Several of Singapore's presidents previously had a career with the labor unions. The party recruited highly capable and dedicated cadres. The government got allies to support its cause, through the power of appointments within the administration, combined with meritocracy and by avoiding nepotism. Civil servants are closely integrated in implementing the government's policy.

Singapore also built bilateral alliances in support of an open multilateral framework. It has been non-aligned with regard to great power rivalries, "seeking to be friends with all who wish to be friends with us."[27] It publicly acknowledges the security umbrella the United States has provided to Southeast Asia, which was an important

27 Minister of Foreign Affairs, S. Jayakumar (1997) quoted in Mauzy and Milne (2002), p. 176.

assurance for American investors at the time of the Cold War. In this connection, Singapore has stressed the economic benefits of the United States fighting in Vietnam by giving other countries in the region time to develop their economies and cope with communist insurgencies, and of American naval power, which continues to keep vital global sea lanes open for trade. Singapore works toward having ASEAN support the economic ascendancy of China and India.

In sum, through long-term strategy and judicious tactics, the PAP government built institutions in support of economic growth over the past four decades. Its strategy was to deliver prosperity and security for all and to be held accountable for promises made. Tactics employed included: channeling collective emotions and reinforcing public values in support of its strategy; shrewd exploitation of opponents' weaknesses combined with coercive authority; using the power of enacting legislation; and building alliances. By 1971, the PAP had consolidated its power. The 12-year period from 1959 to 1971 proved crucial. It laid the basis for the next 35 years. By then, the young tree of Singapore's development strategy was firmly rooted. The impressive later successes in building growth-enhancing institutions and policies were founded on the political economy achievements of those early 12 years.

Six Singapore: Past, Future, and What Other Countries Might learn

An integrated strategy, the foundation of Singapore's success

Singapore's economic development experience has been remarkable. At its core were: budgetary discipline and delayed gratification, policies of efficient allocation through price incentives and market mechanisms, social inclusion by providing economic opportunities, capable and honest government, a long-term vision, and win-win cooperative attitudes, although driving hard bargains. Together, they resulted in economic policies, institutions, and attitudes that mutually reinforced each other and produced an impressive economic development record. Singapore built strong pro-growth institutions over time. These helped ensure good economic policy implementation and underpinned the proximate sources of economic growth: increases in the means of production and higher productivity.

The government intervened by creating conditions for gainful private investment, mainly through MNCs. It helped MNCs thrive by creating rewarding opportunities. Locational advantage and the legacy of entrepôt trade provided favorable initial conditions. But it is good policies that provided the modern communications infrastructure, financial stability, the means to finance the tax incentives, and a competitive labor force. Good institutions ensured social and political stability, and effective and honest government. Sharing the benefits and offering opportunities brought legitimacy. The government took a rational, non-ideological approach: engineering prosperity was the focal point of its policies that pulled in other desirable national goals. The economic growth process created a sense of purpose and community.

The integration of economic outcomes, policies, institutions, and political economy is a recurrent theme in this book. Labor market policies and institutions aptly illustrate the integrated approach that underlies the city-state's successful growth dynamics. The antagonistic labor-employer relations that initially prevailed obstructed the government's vision of growth through foreign investment-based, labor-intensive, export-oriented manufacturing. Only a genuine commitment by the government to create a stake for all, backed up over time by tangible improvements in incomes, health and education for all could earn it the workers' trust and confidence. The government cultivated union relations, confronted residual opposition, and built the supporting legislative and wage-negotiating institutions. Wage flexibility helped ensure efficient allocation. Average real wages rose by just under 5 percent per annum during 1973–97 and full employment prevailed most of the time.[1] In the government's hands, the different pieces were engineered holistically, ultimately to serve labor and the economy as a whole.

Combating corruption is another example of many elements fitting together in a multifaceted approach. Starting at the top; consistent enforcement of stringent anti-corruption legislation regardless of rank; competitive remuneration for a lean civil service for which fiscal policy provided non-inflationary resources, and minimizing economic as well as political opportunities for corruption all reinforced each other. Combined, these various facets produced results beyond what any subset of them might have accomplished. Many heads of state and high-ranking officials have visited Singapore over the years, expressing a wish to "learn from its success" in this and other areas. Often they would pick a few palatable items, as if from a buffet menu, for application in their home country. Leaving key elements out, however, they would miss the synergy, or worse. Picking the high-salary piece, while leaving the high-and well-connected exempt from anti-corruption law could in fact be counterproductive.

1 Lee Kuan Yew (2000), p. 114. Average real wage growth fell to 2.7 percent annually in 1998–2005. Source: Department of Statistics, Singapore.

Housing policy, as designed and fine-tuned over the years, served multiple objectives. It reduced unemployment, created income growth, contributed to ethnic harmony, instilled self-esteem and national allegiance through ownership, beautified the island, and helped build constructive labor relationships. Addressing this binding constraint early on produced multiple favorable effects, killing more than two birds with one stone to use a leftover metaphor from more primitive times. Housing policy, in turn, was intricately intertwined with other specific features of Singapore's policy and institutional set-up such as the CPF and the HDB.

The elusive Singapore label

So far, this book has avoided the phrase "Singapore model." The dictionary defines model as "a standard or example for imitation or comparison." The drawback of the phrase, to my mind, is its connotation with copying specifics, instead of seeking to apply proven principles to each country's unique circumstances. But how do we characterize Singapore's economy? Selecting a single label has proved elusive. Singapore's economy defies easy labeling, since it is full of paradoxes.

Some have called it a capitalist free-market economy. The conservative Heritage Foundation ranks Singapore the second-most free economy in the world, after Hong Kong, for its overall efficient pro-business climate.[2] The World Economic Forum lists Singapore as a "highly competitive economy," ahead of Japan and the United Kingdom in its rankings.[3] Freedom House, by contrast, which focuses on political rights and civil liberties, gives Singapore a poor rating and classifies it as only "partly free."[4] Others have described the PAP rule as "authoritarian capitalism," in contrast with the authoritarian socialism of communist states.[5]

2 Heritage Foundation (2006), *Index of Economic Freedom.*
3 World Economic Forum (2005).
4 Freedom House (2005).
5 Lingle (1996).

Lee Kuan Yew has emphasized the socialist origin: "We believed in socialism, a fair share for all."[6] Descriptors in the literature include: "pragmatic socialism,"[7] "socialism that works,"[8] and "market socialism."[9] Elements of a "planned economy" can be found in the strong interventionism by the government in most economic sectors. Some have labeled Singapore an administrative state that is depoliticized and run by public-minded economic technocrats.[10]

Singapore has been called "a corporate state mainly run by PAP technocrats,"[11] and a "well-run corporation"[12] with a strong balance sheet and that deals responsibly with its various "stakeholders," including the public. Several have emphasized the role of MNCs, including the characterization as "a conglomerate economy dominated by state-sponsored firms that have thrived on collaboration with MNCs."[13] Others have emphasized Singapore's dependence on foreign technology and brain power.

Schein has stressed the "strategic pragmatism"[14] and Low characterized Singapore's economy as "government-made."[15]

Which is correct? To a degree, all of the above. Singapore's economy can be seen as a unique experiment to combine the best of available systems in a flexible, pragmatic, and unorthodox way—suited to its particular circumstances. At the center is a governing elite that has been democratically elected on a mandate of engineering prosperity. Community prevails over individual interests. Society accepts illiberal democracy, preferring to give up some individual rights in exchange for greater prosperity and social stability. The elite needs continuity of policy to implement its long-term vision. A dominant party system, with other political parties

6 Lee Kuan Yew (2000), p. 116.
7 Barr (2000).
8 Goh Keng Swee (1976).
9 Gayle (1988).
10 Seah, C.M. (1999).
11 Huff (1999).
12 Kim (1992).
13 Lian (2000).
14 Schein (1996).
15 Low (1998).

kept purposely weak, shields it from challenges to its power from individuals, the press, and advocacy groups. The latter, "being unelected, cannot expect to set the agenda or have their way about how to run Singapore," as put by Senior Minister Goh Chok Tong.[16] The citizenry, in this view, having exerted their right to elect their governors in regular, fair, and free elections then authorize the governors to act on their behalf.[17] To deliver, the elite must be meritocratic, ensure its constant renewal to maximize talent, and have safeguards against corruption. Effective governance ensures implementation of judicious policies and institutions.

Prospects for Future Growth

Singapore's success cannot be denied. But will the economy continue to grow sufficiently rapidly? Will the social contract hold? Can it last over the long run? In the mid-1990s, Young and Krugman expressed the neo-classical verdict that accumulation of factors of production cannot sustain high growth indefinitely. Huff noted that growth in the Soviet Union slowed dramatically once the upper limits of labor and capital accumulation were reached in the 1960s. The USSR found it impossible to continue to grow despite official directives aimed at decreeing technical progress. Of course, that was a command economy, and also a highly closed society ultimately forced to acknowledge defeat in a costly war in Afghanistan. But economists had sown the seed of doubt about the longevity of Singapore's impressive economic growth record as the economy matured.

Innovativeness and creativity are the lifeblood of growth in advanced economies, warned Michael Porter.[18] To be creative, people's minds need to transcend established rules. Entrepreneurship requires risk-taking. Singapore's environment was not considered

16 Senior Minister Goh Chok Tong, quoted in Mauzy and Milne (2002), p. 168.
17 Schumpeter (1947) called this a minimalist "delegates or elite" model.
18 Porter, reported in the *Straits Times*, August 3, 2001. See also Peebles and Wilson, p. 254, and Porter (1990), p. 566.

conducive to these cultural traits. Years of social conditioning and the stigma attached to failure made Singaporeans reluctant to work in an unfettered environment where the risk is high. The educational system focused on strictly defined curricula and faithful reproduction during written exams, not on capacity for innovation and ability to work independently.[19] Conformity and adherence to rules are not well suited when product design, marketing, and quality service become paramount. The view prevailed that the government itself had nurtured those attitudes. Its strong guidance had discouraged Singaporeans from venturing outside the accepted channels. The heavy hand of the government in the economy was thought to have stifled local entrepreneurial initiative. Many consider Singapore's political future closely tied to continued rapid economic growth. Will the government tolerate the greater individualism and diversity required for creativity and innovation?

The government responded early and strongly to keep the economy globally competitive. In the late 1990s, a high-level committee presented its vision of turning Singapore into an advanced service-oriented and knowledge-intensive global city. The economy had to continue evolving nimbly, ride on regional economic growth, and tap into opportunities from all over the world. Improved productivity in manufacturing and diversification was essential to maintain a competitive edge, with further expansion of advanced engineering training. Another idea was to develop niches of excellence and creating the conditions for "clusters" of activity to flourish, in tourism, healthcare, tertiary education, financial services, biomedical sciences, and most recently digital and interactive media and water management technologies. Gross expenditure on R&D rose steadily to 2.3 percent of GDP in 2004 and is targeted to rise further to 3 percent by 2010.[20] Singapore's transformation into a culturally vibrant cosmopolitan city-state, with the kind of excitement one finds in London or New York, should support the

19 Huff (1999).
20 Budget speech by Prime Minister Lee, February 17, 2006.

attraction of global talent. Venture capital facilities support innovative local entrepreneurs. The government urges local firms to strive to become world-class operators. The public school curriculum, at all levels, is being revised to give more emphasis to problem solving and creative thinking to help students compete in the knowledge economy. As expressed by one source: "Daring and passion are gradually added to the traditional roster of discipline and perseverance."[21] Nonetheless, although the utilitarian market-based approach is loosened up slightly, Singapore's education does not yet have the creativity, curiosity, sense of adventure, or ambition that can be found in cultures where learning challenges conventional wisdom and authority.

Singapore's medium-term potential economic growth for the period until 2020 is expected to decelerate to 4.5–5 percent per year. MAS economists project a range from 4.1 percent to 5.8 percent, depending on TFP growth.[22] A recent study by IMF staff, which we discussed in Chapter 1, projects 4.5 percent as a base-case scenario *on average* over the next 15 years (see Figure 6.1).[23] This projected outcome is between the actual rates of growth achieved in 1990–2003 respectively by Singapore (6.2 percent), and by a sample of industrial countries (2.5 percent). Singapore's growth is expected to decelerate, because of slower expansion in the labor force and a decline in the investment ratio. This baseline projection assumes that education levels and skills continue to rise at the same rate observed during the most recent decade, and that TFP growth maintains its average of the past 43 years.[24] Bilateral free trade and cooperation agreements as well as the numerous government initiatives under way aimed at switching to higher-growth niches—such as establishing a global education hub for 150,000 students by 2012 or major new tourist

21 Insight Guide (2000).
22 Monetary Authority of Singapore (2000), pp. 20–21.
23 Eggertsson (2004).
24 As discussed in Chapter 1, the study estimated that TFP growth contributed 1.4 percentage points to Singapore's average rate of growth of 7.7 percent during 1960–2003.

Figure 6.1 Singapore: Future Sources of Growth

	Annual Growth (In percent)		
	Singapore (1990-2003)	**Singapore projected** (2004-2020)	**Industrial countries** (1990-2003)
Labor	1.8	1.4	1.0
Capital	7.5	4.0	3.1
Education	1.3	1.3	0.3
GDP Growth	6.2	4.5	2.5
Contribution of			
Labor	1.2	0.9	0.6
Capital	2.6	1.4	1.1
Education	0.8	0.8	0.2
TFP	1.6	1.4	0.5

Source: Eggertsson (2004).

attractions—would contribute to TFP growth. It should be noted that the above exercise focuses on GDP. One might expect GNI to grow faster than GDP, in the event that Singapore continues to register external current account surpluses on the order of 15 percent of GDP or higher over the medium term, as this would rapidly raise Singapore's net foreign assets.

Some political scientists and observers doubt that the above scenario will play out as favorably as projected. Singapore's culture of control and suppression of dissent has long been decried. In their view, Singapore does not qualify as an open society.[25] As economic growth shifts from investment based to innovation driven, a different set of attitudes is required that have been languishing in a state-controlled environment. Growing affluence is likely to lead more people to claim the right to dissent and to clamor for contest of

25 On January 11, 2006, renowned financier George Soros observed that Singapore was not an open society because the use of libel suits against opposition politicians curbs the freedom of expression.

political power. The social contract could be undermined. Samuel Huntington is of the view that after Lee Kuan Yew's retirement from public life: "the political system will degenerate and decay as corruption sets in...The efficiency and honesty that Lee Kuan Yew has brought to Singapore will follow him to the grave."[26] In his view, history has shown that benevolent authoritarians succumb due to the absence of adequate feedback mechanisms and institutions of self-reform, including public debate, a free press, protest movements, and competitive elections involving opposition parties. Only if civil society asserts itself and exerts control can government be kept disciplined and law-abiding. This same thesis was expressed earlier by CV Devan Nair, a former president of Singapore who later became a severe critic of the government.[27] He wrote in 1994 that the "loutish political style of the PAP is not compatible with continued economic growth." Growth has continued, however. Equally, Huntington's words were barely spoken or Prime Minister Goh Chok Tong rallied the nation to turn this dire prediction into a self-denying prophecy, true to the tradition of molding any adversity into a new opportunity to progress.[28] In his opposite view, critical self-renewal of Singapore's leadership is possible without adversarial outside pressure groups.

26 Huntington (1996) and the *Business Times*, May 29, 2000. See http://www.singapore-windo.org/sw00/000529bt.htm.

27 CV Devan Nair (1994). Singapore's third president emigrated to Canada where he passed away in 2005. He played a major role during three decades in making the labor unions a partner in the PAP's development strategy.

28 Prime Minister's National Day Rally Speech 1999, Singapore: Ministry of Information and the Arts, 1999, p. 53. Quoted in Mauzy and Milne (2002), p. 186.

Political openness

"To develop, a country needs discipline more than democracy in the Western sense."

Lee Kuan Yew[29]

"We prize our values...but sometimes we judge every other state by the criteria of our own civilization."

Henry Kissinger[30]

Singapore has been characterized as an "illiberal" democracy. As one political scientist said: "The government in Singapore stands out as insisting on exclusive political control in an economically developed polity."[31] Singapore's elite proudly believes in the right to shape the specific organizational forms of its political institutions in light of its own circumstances and timing and is comfortable justifying them.[32] Political institutions, such as universal suffrage, in Western countries evolved over many decades. Full-fledged Western style democracy, in this view, is favored but will be introduced only progressively, along with the development of an established and educated middle class.[33] The belief of Singapore's leadership in the benefits, for now, of one-party dominance explains its attitude toward the opposition and the media. The media and opposition politicians, in the government's view, serve their own agenda through actions that risk contributing to popular dissatisfaction and foment fiscal irresponsibility. The economic strategy pursued hinges on collective fiscal discipline sustained over decades that lets society benefit from the power of

29 Lee Kuan Yew, Manila, November 1992, quoted in McGurn (1993).
30 Kissinger, Henry in 'Foreword' Lee Kuan Yew (2000).
31 Rodan (1997).
32 Mahbubani (2002), p. 48.
33 This is in line with Gunnar Myrdal (1968), p. 773: Despite Myrdal's personal attachment to liberal democracy and his awareness that many in Asia strongly favor it, empirical observation led him to conclude that it was not essential for development. "True, for development to occur a regime should be in accord with the interests of the people and should be willingly accepted by the great majority. It should also permit general freedom of thought and action, even if it engages in some suppression of public opposition and does not condone the observation of the full range of civil liberties."

compounding. As a result, Singapore has been highly successful. In the government's view, key criticisms leveled at it risk undermining the economic strategy by upsetting its internal coherence and social order and therefore overall well-being. Siren songs (for example, unconditional needs-based welfare provisions) that focus on only one limited aspect of a complex reality must not tempt Singapore to stop pursuing its destiny and be distracted by secondary goals. Smooth transitions of leadership in 1990 and 2004—the current prime minister is the son of Lee Kuan Yew—help ensure continuity of policies, thus reducing uncertainty for investors.[34]

Many reject these views. Amartya Sen, 1998 Nobel Laureate for Economics, pleads for declaring democracy a "universal" value. He said: "A country does not have to become fit for democracy; it has to become fit *through* democracy."[35] He stresses three reasons. First, political participation and freedom have intrinsic importance in human life, as evidenced by people opting for democracy wherever they are offered a choice; second, because experience in countries such as India demonstrates the need for effective democratic opposition and full civil liberties, including the right to protest and a free press, to make governments respond to the needs of the poor—in the historic case of India to prevent famine—and keep them accountable for their financial management; and third, because of the constructive role of unrestricted interactive debate by competing protagonists in an effective democratic forum for the formation of people's values and in the understanding of their needs, rights, and duties. Sen also notes that empirical evidence about a tradeoff between economic performance and democracy is indeterminate:

34 While dynastic succession conjures up suspicions of nepotism, Lee Hsien Loong had impressive credentials of his own prior to becoming prime minister, including a distinguished military career (he rose to brigadier-general), academic degrees from top international institutions, and experience spanning over a decade as deputy prime minister with responsibilities in a range of areas, including chairman of MAS and finance minister.

35 Sen (1999).

Figure 6.2 Democracy and GDP per Capita

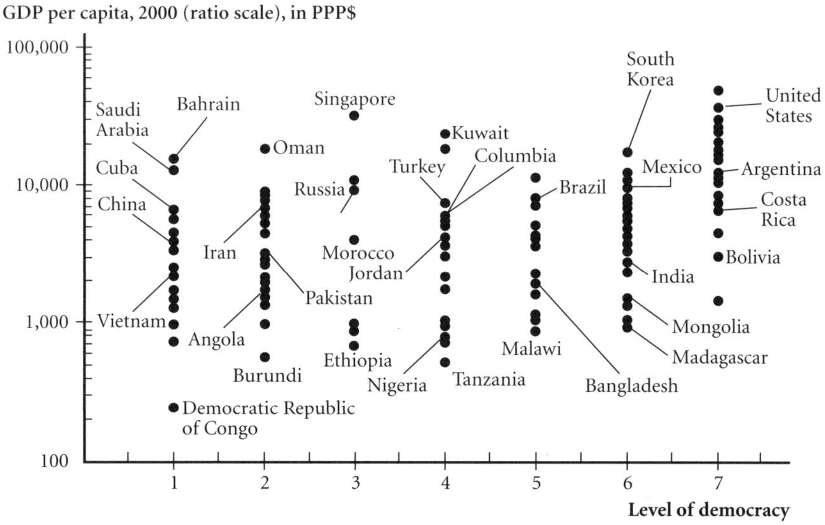

Source: Weil, D. (2005), Figure 12.6, p. 359, based on Freedom House (2001). ©2005 Pearson Education, Inc. Reprinted with permission.

democracies include stellar economic performers such as Botswana but others with a bad economic record; authoritarian regimes count Singapore as a success but many are dismal failures.

Figure 6.2 depicts the statistical relationship between the degree of democracy, measured by political rights (competitiveness of the political system and the accountability of its leaders) and the *level* of per capita income. The data are on a 7-point scale with 1 being the least democratic, and are based on the classification of countries in this presentation by Freedom House for 2000.[36] Richer countries tend to be more democratic but the direction of causation is not self-evident. Probably richer countries ask more democracy: South Korea over time traveled in the northeast direction in the scatter diagram.

36 This paragraph is based on David Weil (2005). Some in Singapore dispute the country's ranking. Also, it may be pointed out that relating Freedom House indicators of democracy for one particular year (2000) to income levels in that same year may be time-inconsistent if political regimes in some countries were very different in preceding years.

But the statistical relationship is not a strong one. As noted also by Robert Barro (1997), democracy neither helps nor hinders growth: regressing economic *growth* against indicators of the rule of law, free markets, low government consumption, high human capital formation, and initial GDP per capita level leaves the impact of democracy as an additional variable negative but statistically weak. The impact of democracy is ambiguous, as Weil points out: On the positive side, democracies and political freedom put limits on the worst forms of rulers including kleptocrats and autocrats. But democracies can also be prone to political instability and to short-term calculations that sacrifice long-term economic growth for short-term electoral expediency. High taxes for redistribution purposes can create disincentives and promote inefficiency, which harm growth. In the view of Barro, the optimal level of democracy, from an economic growth point of view, is about in the middle of the scale. If his analysis is correct, democracy is a luxury good that wealthy countries choose, even if it reduces income.[37]

On the issue of press freedom, Singapore and the West do not see eye to eye. Freedom House declared that the press is not free in Singapore: journalists practice self-censorship rather than risk being charged under the country's harsh criminal defamation laws. Circulation of foreign periodicals has been restricted for publishing news that interferes with domestic policies. Prominent journalists over many years have repeatedly denounced Lee Kuan Yew as a dictator like Saddam Hussein.[38]

As a sovereign country with an elected government and Parliament, Singapore considers it has a mandate to set its own laws regarding the press that differ from Western values and preferences. The PAP government challenges the premise that where the media is free, the market place of ideas sorts the irresponsible and erroneous from what is responsible and correct and rewards the latter within an acceptable timeframe. The necessity of an unfettered press as a public

37 Barro (1997), quoted in Weil (2005), p. 358; see also Barro (1994).
38 Lee Kuan Yew (2000), p. 225.

good in order to achieve good governance is rejected in Singapore's case, given the country's strong record on public integrity. The government insists on the right to have its replies printed in its own words, if it considers that newspapers report facts erroneously. A long-held view of the Singapore leadership is that the business interests of newspaper owners lead them to influence the hearts and minds of their readers—Singapore voters—by presenting their own point of view and thereby affect internal politics. One concern is that unfettered press freedom could inflame civil strife by sensationalizing and exploiting racial, ethnic, or religious issues. Power over the hearts and minds of the electorate is at issue. In Lee Kuan Yew's words: "In a young country like Singapore, I need the media to reinforce, not to undermine, the cultural values and social attitudes. Freedom of the press must be subordinated to the overriding needs of Singapore, and to the primacy of purpose of an elected government." While this narrows the editorial spectrum since the press is not allowed to be confrontational, it need not preclude high-quality debate, which does take place. Moreover, the government feels that it must challenge erroneous press reports, if needed in court, lest it lose respect and therefore power with the electorate.[39] Leadership must be resolute or fades away.[40] Nonetheless, as Lee realized: "With the rise of the internet...we cannot and should not stop the foreign voices now. But the views of the government of Singapore on major issues must be known to Singaporeans."

39 Courts have been criticized for being highly formalistic in their interpretation of the laws as enacted by Parliament, and in that sense independent only to a degree.

40 Leifer (2000), pp. 8–9 observes that Singapore has been determined to assert its right to decide its own future, and that this has meant a "don't flinch" mentality (internationally and domestically) of not showing any weaknesses, while at the same time displaying its political resolve at every opportunity. Commenting on nuances within this approach, Rajaratnam allegedly observed: "Goh (Chok Tong) is flexible but it is a flexibility of steel...whereas Lee Kuan Yew is titanium, stiff. Anybody who bangs against titanium breaks his head." Quoted in Mutalib (2000), p. 322.

CHALLENGES AHEAD

Singapore's government continuously scans the horizon for new clouds that might disturb economic growth or threaten social stability. Challenges to the country's competitive position in a rapidly globalizing world are addressed on an ongoing basis in the government's evolving economic plans, strategies, and budgets. China and India rank high among those concerns since their ascendancy compels Singapore to restructure continuously to maintain full employment. On the positive side, both countries' economic dynamism also offers prospects for decreasing dependency on the U.S. economy over time. Keeping ASEAN on track toward its ambitious project to create an economic union by 2015 and thereby leverage its geographic position to intermediate between China and India, as the region has done historically, is part of Singapore's geopolitical strategy.

A different challenge closer to home is to keep Singapore as an inclusive society. Singapore's people are its resource, their well-being the end-goal of policy. But who are the inhabitants? Centrifugal forces will impact the size and composition of the future labor force and population. Birth rates have declined as women have appealing career choices. Emigration does occur, as Singapore's talented young have options abroad. The optimal size for the population has been put at around 6 million. Singapore would seem well placed to attract working-age immigrants, as it can compete for talent abroad and offer attractive terms. The foreign labor component, estimated at about 30 percent, is expected to rise further. The Biopolis, the huge medical science hub, is meant to attract thousands of brilliant minds. Will Singapore be a thriving global city only for a transient foreign elite or for the local population as well? Their permanency of stay would seem vital in giving Singapore an identity and a soul.

Here lies one potential area of friction as older unskilled workers interpret foreign arrivals as the cause of their more difficult job market conditions. Income gaps are likely to rise between a meritocratic upper income group with conspicuous lifestyles and those struggling at the bottom, which the government is determined to prevent from falling into a permanent underclass. Ethnicity could also surface as an issue if minority groups consider their economic opportunities diminished, including as a result of being disadvantaged with regard to Chinese language proficiency, which China's ascent may put at a premium. The proud heritage of Islamic schools in promoting Muslim learning continues to attract youngsters from Singapore's 15 percent Malay/Muslim community, but learning Quranic exegesis and Arabic might not help them enter a competitive job market. Singapore's population will age rapidly from 2015, barring stepped-up immigration or a reversal of declining birth rates. As the government has stated, staying ahead for Singapore will also require staying together and not leaving some vulnerable citizens behind.

The political environment is another challenge. Singapore is an outlier, statistically. In several of the scatter diagrams in this book, it occupies an unexpected corner given its high per capita income level. As one observer expressed: "Singapore's economy is improbably state-dominated; its policies remain improbably undemocratic, despite First World levels of wealth and education enjoyed by Singaporeans."[41] There is a juxtaposition between the government's remarkable openness to ideas from around the world and its aversion to public dissent. The PAP fiercely resists challenges to its power, a trait that goes back to the early fights for survival. With growing affluence, however, along with top-notch education, international exposure, and increased confidence, more Singaporeans will wish to form their own opinions through more open political discourse on how to organize their collective lives, even if they prefer not to enter party politics. More people may insist on the space and opportunity to dissent, even if they choose to conform. The elders have created a magnificent home but the younger generation may wish to redecorate it, or else strike out on their own or drift into consumerism or apathy.

41 Wilkin (2004).

The PAP government recognizes the need for greater openness as long as its power is not threatened. As Lee Hsien Loong said when he was deputy prime minister: “The combination of a vibrant civil society and strong government will not be easy to achieve. As long as the argument is over policies, the limits for debate…are very wide…and there is no subject taboo…But if it is an attack on the government’s fitness to rule…that has to address a broader question.”[42] For the PAP, the challenge seems to be how to loosen some of the political boundaries without appearing to be weak or succumb to confrontation, how to enter a more trusting relationship with civil society without risking descent into disorder, how to give voice in a more pluralistic political setting without signaling the beginning of the end of the Singapore system.

Disagreeing over values is legitimate in modern societies. People’s inter-temporal preferences differ: some relish saving, others spending in the present. Core issues of policy including the future course of saving and investment, the role of the external economy, the pace of GLC divestment, and the strategy on immigration are legitimate issues for political discussion on the tradeoffs involved. Is the continued presence of the state in many levels of life necessary for political stability and economic growth? In such debates, Singapore’s younger generation will likely have a keen interest in how the older leadership can translate the hard-learnt and very real lessons of past decades into actual 21st century reality, without amplifying looming risks. This would be all the more important if other Asian economies perform well, while handling the frailties of their own ethnic and religious fault lines with greater popular participation in politics. As the electorate becomes more complex, so will the government. Values and practices will not stay immutable in Singapore, even if norms espoused by others are not adopted. Open debate already takes place on issues such as draft dodging, casinos in Singapore, and corporate governance in charities such as the NKF, but not on the competence

42 *Straits Times Weekly Edition*, January 17, 2000, quoted in Mauzy and Milne (2002), p. 167.

and integrity of political personalities in positions of authority.[43] In the words of Cabinet Minister Dr Vivian Balakrishnan, on issues of political freedom, Singapore will be "cautiously radical" rather than "ideologically revolutionary."[44]

Availability of reliable information will improve the quality of public discourse. The government has increasingly released valuable information in recent years. The public review of Temasek Holdings' operations in its first ever annual report released on October 2004 offered welcome transparency.[45] Demand will probably continue to increase for public disclosure about the affairs of the state, including its macro-finances. Greater transparency on transactions related to the balance sheet of the government, income earned on public investments, including of GLCs, and consolidated accounts of the public sector in line with international accounting standards would enhance understanding of Singapore's economy.[46] More information could be shared with the public without endangering strategic interests of GLCs in a competitive world or revealing market-sensitive information or burdening civil servants to meet data requests. Increased disclosure may facilitate operations of GLCs abroad and reassure investors about financial performance and soundness, as was the case following the Temasek report. The stakes keep growing, as surpluses continue to accumulate in the balance of

43 A high salary of the CEO of the National Kidney Foundation (NKF), a charitable Institute of Public Character (IPC), combined with lavish expenses and inadequate oversight by the Board of Directors of ethical conduct, resulted in a scandal in early 2006 that dented the country's reputation for corporate governance.

44 *Strait Times*, January 13, 2006.

45 Contrary to its principal companies, Temasek Holdings itself is not listed on the Singapore Exchange and not required to disclose its financial accounts. See John Burton, "Temasek sets itself high standards," *Financial Times*, October 14, 2004; also, Temasek's latest review at http://www.temasekholdings.com.sg/2005review.

46 The Government of Singapore Investment Corporation (GIC) is the largest investment company in Singapore. It manages Singapore's assets by investing abroad in equities, fixed income and money market instruments, and real estate. Assets managed by the GIC have reportedly grown to more than US$100 billion, but details of its investments have not been made public (IMF (2004), p. 36). GIC-RE manages about one-tenth of GIC's assets and is one of the world's top 10 real-estate investment companies. GIC is organized as a private company even though it is wholly owned by the Ministry of Finance and is not subject to corporate disclosure laws.

payments and the government budget when measured inclusively. These public funds have been amassed through strenuous saving by ordinary people. The elite responsible for managing them are conscious of their fiduciary responsibility, and there is no reason to doubt that they act as true trustees. Nonetheless, trust in their expert competence and high moral character and in the existence of adequate internal checks and balances need not preclude public accountability of performance. As the public grows increasingly sophisticated, including on financial matters, greater disclosure would contribute to more informed discussion on the direction of economic policy by a larger segment of the polity. This would be in line with trends in corporate finance, including in Singapore, where increased disclosure has reinforced regulatory regimes and enhanced accountability.

Singapore's macro-finances, and its development model in general, are remarkably strong and coherent. The government can credibly defend all its major aspects. The high saving has served the country well. Disclosing its full magnitude and details on its composition need not erode support for fiscal conservatism.[47] The rapidly rising saving ratio was matched by a steady decline in the share of private consumption in GDP, falling from 77 percent of GDP in 1966 to as low as 40 percent in 1999, reflecting the growing importance of investment and net exports in aggregate expenditure.[48] This consumption ratio is low compared to any developed country. Singapore's citizens accepted consumption of a shrinking share of GDP as long as the total pie grew rapidly enough for the absolute size of a worker's slice of it to continue to increase. That has been the case

47 This assertion is at variance with the view of Goh Keng Swee, Singapore's principal economic architect, who argued in 1965 that, since economic growth demands much sacrifice from the people, most of them would never want to go through it even if they were guaranteed long-term prosperity in return. Source: *Strait Times*, July 26, 1965, quoted in Mutalib (2000), p. 317.

48 Peebles and Wilson (2002), p. 78. The private consumption ratio rose to 43 percent in 2004–05. The concept needs to be interpreted with caution since the "private" sector in the national income statistics includes public corporations.

indeed: real consumption per Singapore labor force member (in 1990 S$) rose from S$10,000 in 1967 to S$26,400 by 1997, a compound rate of 3.3 percent annually.[49] A majority of the populace will likely agree that fiscal prudence was justified in view of Singapore's many vulnerabilities and uncertainties, such as risks of losing manufacturing MNCs to lower-cost countries, regional upheaval and security threats, global recession or epidemics, and in the long run possibly rising sea-levels. Wise policies have equipped Singapore better than many advanced societies to confront future challenges of an aging population and structural unemployment.

Outsiders will follow developments in Singapore with interest. When peering into the future, circumstances prevailing now in 2006 serve as initial conditions for any forward looking exercise. How will Singapore evolve over the next 15 years? The government will likely perfect the existing model, whereby a meritocratic technocracy leads society. It will do everything in its power to keep the economy humming, and in the process, keep Singapore a fascinating place, while seeking to balance the need to secure the country's economic fortune with longer-run concerns about identity and authenticity. Singaporeans would seem to be eminently well equipped to face the challenges of the future, having a solid base of values and an economic record of success that gives self-confidence. In the view of Linda Low: "Singaporeans are very pragmatic and down-to-earth. They will not roll back the PAP's achievements."[50] A modern, educated, and sophisticated electorate may remain surprisingly conformist. Barring a steep world recession or unforeseen calamity, the forecast would seem to be for more, or under the circumstances even better, of the same: a sustainable economic growth rate on the order of 5 percent on average, continued further qualitative development, and broadening the model for greater involvement of the citizenry.

---

49 Huff (1999), p. 44. Recalculated for 1970–2004, this rate of growth fell to 2.8 percent annually on average.
50 Low (1998), p. 271.

What other countries might learn

Friends in a hurry asked if I could summarize the book for them in one sentence: Singapore engineered prosperity through enlightened strategy. My hope, however, is that readers have found useful insights for other countries throughout the book while taking into account their own specific circumstances. In the words of Woodrow Wilson to his American compatriots: "As a nation, we can never learn either our own weaknesses or our own virtues by comparing ourselves with ourselves." And, after studying other cultures: "We took to rice, but we do not eat with chopsticks."[51]

Key themes emerged from Singapore's story. These include: the role of saving in allowing the buildup of first-rate infrastructure; the growth potential of increased labor force participation and immigration; the central importance of economic development among national goals; sharing opportunities for growth widely to make people more productive through better health and education; the macroeconomic resilience and employment-creating potential provided by flexible wage policy; competent civil service and integrity of governance; fiscal discipline and setting aside surpluses during boom years; win-win relations with MNCs and labor; maintaining racial harmony; learning from others pragmatically; the rule of law; and well-designed policies. I also believe that the template developed in this book—moving from economic growth outcomes and their proximate causes, to initial conditions, policies, institutions, and the political economy of implementation—provides a useful framework for analyzing the economic growth experience of other countries, with Singapore serving as a benchmark for comparison. To conclude, three lessons can be highlighted.

First, Singapore followed an integrated approach to development. Outcomes, policies, institutions, social and cultural values, and the political dynamics of implementation all reinforced each other. The

---

51 Wilson (1887).

government pursued this comprehensive strategy across a range of areas such as fiscal, monetary policy, education, health, transportation, housing, finance, wage policy, legal system and law enforcement, labor markets, and political stability and legitimacy. The result was an intricate network of mutually reinforcing linkages producing a powerful outcome.

A second theme that emerged throughout was the distinction between basic principles or core functions, such as a stable currency or accountable and responsive government, and their specific application in the context of a given country. Each country must sequence its own development path. Good institutions can take a variety of forms. Each country must fashion the specifics of its policies and institutions tailored to its own local geographical and historical conditions, while keeping to general principles that have proved to be robust over time and across countries. But there is no flexibility on the need for consistent steps forward over many decades to get a solidly successful result, as Singapore's experience illustrates.

Third, leadership is imperative for effective governance. The argument that institutions are crucial to development but are deeply rooted in history and difficult to change need not lead to excessive pessimism. It is true that Figure 1.1 in Chapter 1 with the negative economic growth rates for a number of countries over the past 40 years, and their seeming inability to put in place growth-enhancing policies and institutions can be depressing. Without belittling the obstacles that these countries face, that pessimism need not be justified. Institutions have changed for the better in a number of countries over the past 40 years. Learning and sharing insight is possible and does take place. Singapore succeeded because its leadership was assiduous, highly intelligent in a practical way, determined to achieve shared prosperity, and committed to act with integrity. Leading with vision and fortitude is possible. Its benefits can be invaluable. That is Singapore's ultimate lesson.

Bibliography

Acemoglu, Daron, Simon Johnson, and James A. Robinson (2004). "Institutions as the Fundamental Cause of Long-Run Growth," in Philippe Aghion and Steven Durlauf, (eds.), *Handbook of Economic Growth.* Amsterdam: North Holland.

Asher, Mukul (2002). "Reforming Singapore's Tax System for the twenty-first century," in Koh Ai Tee et al. (eds.), *Singapore Economy in the 21st Century: Issues and Strategies.* Singapore: McGraw-Hill Education.

Asher, Mukul (2004). "Retirement Financing Dilemmas: Experience of Singapore," *Economic and Political Weekly*, Vol. XXXIX, No. 21, pp. 2114–20.

Austin, Ian Patrick (2004). *Goh Keng Swee and Southeast Asian Governance.* Singapore: Marshall Cavendish Academic.

Barr, Michael D. (2000), *Lee Kuan Yew: The Beliefs behind the Man*. Washington, DC: Georgetown University Press.

Barro, Robert (1997). *Determinants of Economic Growth: A Cross-Country Empirical Study.* Cambridge, MA: MIT Press.

Bercuson, Kenneth (ed.) (1995). "Singapore: A Case Study in Rapid Development," IMF Occasional Paper No. 119. Washington, DC: International Monetary Fund.

Cardarelli, Roberto (2000), "Singapore's Central Provident Fund: Options for a Comprehensive Reform," *Singapore: Selected Issues,* IMF Staff Country Report No. 00/83, Washington, DC: International Monetary Fund, pp. 53–67.

Chee Soon Juan (2001). *Your Future, My Faith, Our Freedom: A Democratic Blueprint for Singapore.* Singapore: Open Singapore Centre.

Chew, Melanie (1996). *Leaders of Singapore.* Singapore: Resource Press.

Chin, Anthony T.H. (2002). "Urban Growth and a Sustainable Environment: Land transportation initiatives and traffic congestion," in Koh Ai Tee et al. (eds.), *Singapore Economy in the 21st Century: Issues and Strategies.* Singapore: McGraw-Hill Education.

Department of Statistics, Singapore, at http://www.singstat.gov.sg.

Eggertsson, Gauti, "Medium-Term Growth Prospects," in IMF (2004), *Singapore: Selected Issues*, IMF Staff Country Report No. 04/103. Washington, DC: International Monetary Fund, pp. 5–14.

Freedom House (2005). Freedom of the Press 2004, at http://www.freedomhouse.org/research.

Gayle, Dennis John (1988). "Singaporean market socialism: Some implications for development theory," *International Journal of Social Economics,* 15 (7).

George, Cherian (2000). *Singapore: The Air-Conditioned Nation—Essays on the Politics of Comfort and Control, 1990–2000.* Singapore: Landmark Books.

Ghesquiere, Rik (1976). *Tussen Eden en Utopia—Ontwikkeling in Zuid-oost Azie.* Leuven: Davidsfonds.

Goh Keng Swee (1976). "A socialist economy that works," in C.V. Devan Nair (ed.), *Socialism that Works: The Singapore Way.* Singapore, Kuala Lumpur, Hong Kong: Federal Publications.

Hausmann, Ricardo, Dani Rodrik, and Andres Velasco (2004). "Growth Diagnostics," John F. Kennedy School of Government, Harvard University, at http://ksghome.harvard.edu/~drodrik/barcelonasep20.pdf.

Heritage Foundation (2006). "Index of Economic Freedom," at http://www.heritage.org/research/features/index.

Heston, Alan, Robert Summers, and Bettina Aten (2002). *Penn World Table Version 6.1.* Center for International Comparisons at the University of Pennsylvania (October).

Hsieh Chang-Tai (2002). "What Explains the Industrial Revolution in East Asia? Evidence from the Factor Markets," *American Economic Review*, June, pp. 502–26.

Huff, W.G. (1999). "Singapore's Economic Development: Four Lessons and Some Doubts." *Oxford Development Studies,* Vol. 27(1): pp. 33–55.

Hu, Richard, Parliamentary Debates, Singapore, Vol. 70, No. 18 (August 17, 1999) cols. 2018–31.

Hui Weng Tat (2002). *Foreign manpower policy in Singapore*, in Koh Ai Tee et al. (eds.), *Singapore Economy in the 21st Century: Issues and Strategies.* Singapore: McGraw-Hill Education.

Huntington, Samuel P. (1996). "Democracy for the Long Haul," *Journal of Democracy* 7.2 (1996), pp. 3–13.

Husain, Ishrat (1999). *Pakistan: The Economy of an Elitist State.* Karachi: Oxford University Press.

Insight Guides (2000). *Singapore—Insight Guide*, ninth edition. Singapore: Apa Productions GmbH & Co. Verlag KG.

Institute for Management Development (2001). *World Competitiveness Yearbook, 2001*, at http://www.imd/ch/wcy.

International Monetary Fund. *International Financial Statistics*, various issues. Washington, DC: International Monetary Fund.

International Monetary Fund (2004). *Singapore—Financial System Stability Assessment.* IMF Country Report No 04/104, at http://www.imf.org/external/pubs/ft/scr/2004/cr04/04.pdf.

International Monetary Fund (2005), *Singapore—Staff Report for the 2004 Article IV Consultation.* Washington, DC: International Monetary Fund, at http://www.imf.org/external/pubs/ft/scr/2005/cr05141.pdf.

Jang, Byung K., and Shinichi Nakabayashi (2005). "Some Issues in Medium-Term Fiscal Policy," in *Singapore—Selected Issues*, IMF Country Report 05/140. Washington, DC: International Monetary Fund (April).

Kaufmann, Daniel, Aart Kraay, and Pablo Zoido-Lobatón (2002). "Governance Matters II—Updated Indicators for 2000–01." Mimeo, World Bank.

Keynes, John Maynard (1930). "Economic Possibilities for Our Grandchildren," Repr. in *The Collected Writings of John Maynard Keynes*, Vol. 9, Essays in Persuasion. London: Macmillan (1972).

Kim S.P. (1992). "Singapore in 1991," *Asian Survey*, Vol. 32, pp. 119–25.

Koh, Winston (2005). "Singapore's Economic Growth Experience," in *The Economic Prospects of Singapore*. Singapore: Addison-Wesley.

Krugman, Paul (1994). "The Myth of Asia's Miracle." *Foreign Affairs*, Vol. 73, November-December, pp. 62–78.

Land Transport Authority, Singapore (2004). *Singapore Land Transport Statistics in brief*, at http://www.lta.gov.sg/corp_info/doc/Statistic%20.

Landes, David S. (1999). *The Wealth and Poverty of Nations*. New York: W.W. Norton & Company.

Lee Hsien Loong (1998). "Singapore of the Future" in Arun Mahizhnan and Lee Tsao Yuan (eds.), *Singapore: Re-Engineering Success*. Singapore: Institute of Policy Studies and Oxford University Press.

Lee Kuan Yew (1998). *The Singapore Story: Memoirs of Lee Kuan Yew*. Singapore: Singapore Press Holdings.

Lee Kuan Yew (2000). *From Third World to First: The Singapore Story 1965–2000.* Singapore: Singapore Press Holdings.

Leifer, Michael (2000). *Singapore's Foreign Policy: Coping with Vulnerability*. London: Routledge.

Lian D. (2000). *Singapore: Singapore Inc—New Economy Patron or Old Economy Saint?* at http://www.morganstanley.com/GEFdata/digests/20000605-mon.html#anchor5.

Lim Chong Yah (1996). *Economic Policy Management in Singapore.* Singapore: Addison-Wesley.

Lim Chong Yah (1998). "The national wages council: Targets and goals," in Lim Chong Yah and Rosalind Chew (eds.). *Wages and Wages Policies: Tripartism in Singapore*. Singapore: World Scientific Publishing Co. Pte. Ltd.

Lim Chong Yah (2004). *Southeast Asia: The Long Road Ahead,* second edition. Singapore: World Scientific Publishing Co. Pte. Ltd.

Lim Chong Yah and Associates (1988). *Policy Options for the Singapore Economy.* Singapore: McGraw-Hill Book Co.

Lingle, C. (1996). *Singapore's Authoritarian Capitalism: Asian Values, Free Market Illusions, and Political Dependency.* Barcelona and Fairfax: Ediciones Sirocco and the Locke Institute.

Low, Linda (1998). *The Political Economy of a City-State: Government-made Singapore.* Singapore: Oxford University Press.

Mauzy, Diane K. and R.S. Milne (2002). *Singapore Politics: Under the People's Action Party.* London: Routledge.

Mahbubani, Kishore (2002). *Can Asians think? Understanding the Divide between East and West.* Singapore: Random House Inc.

McGurn, William (1993). Asian Dilemmas, in *National Review*, November 29.

Ministry of Trade and Industry, Singapore (1991). *The Strategic Economic Plan: Toward a Developed Nation.* Singapore: Economic Planning Committee, Ministry of Trade and Industry.

Monetary Authority of Singapore (2000), *Quarterly Bulletin*, Vol. II, No. 4. Singapore: Monetary Authority of Singapore, Economics Department (December).

Monetary Authority of Singapore (2003), *Monetary Policy Operations in Singapore.* Singapore: Monetary Authority of Singapore, at http://www.sgs.gov.sg/publications/download/SGPMonetaryPolicyOperations.pdf.

Monetary Authority of Singapore (2004). "Singapore's Balance of Payments, 1965 to 2003: An Analysis," Occasional Paper No. 33. Singapore: Monetary Authority of Singapore, Economics Department.

Montesquieu, Charles de Secondat, Baron de (1758). *L'Esprit des Lois*, Translated into English by Thomas Nugent (1914) as *The Spirit of Laws*, at http://www.constitution.org/cm/sol.htm.

Mukhopadhaya, Pundarik and Bhanoji Rao (2002). "Income Inequality," in Koh Ai Tee et al. (eds.), *Singapore Economy in the 21st Century: Issues and Strategies.* Singapore: McGraw-Hill Education.

Mutalib, Husin (2000). "Illiberal Democracy and the Future of Opposition in Singapore," *Third World Quarterly*, Vol. 21, No. 2, pp. 313–42.

Myrdal, Gunnar (1968). *Asian Drama: An Inquiry into the Poverty of Nations.* London: Penguin Books.

Nair, C.V. Devan (1994). "Foreword," in Francis T. Seow, *To Catch a Tartar: A Dissident in Lee Kuan Yew's Prison.* Yale Southeast Asia Studies Monograph No. 42. New Haven: Yale Center for International and Area Studies.

North, Douglas C. (1990). *Institutions, Institutional Change and Economic Performance.* New York: Cambridge University Press.

North, Douglas C. (1991). "Institutions," *Journal of Economic Perspectives* 5(1): pp. 97–112.

Parrado, Eric (2004). "Singapore's Unique Monetary Policy: How Does It Work?" IMF Working Paper 04/10. Washington DC: International Monetary Fund.

Peebles, G. and P. Wilson (1996). *The Singapore Economy*, Cheltenham: Edward Elgar.

Peebles, G. and P. Wilson (2002). *Economic Growth and Development in Singapore: Past and Future.* Cheltenham, UK; Northampton, MA: Edward Elgar.

Peebles, G. and P. Wilson (2004). "The Economic Vulnerability and Resilience of Small Island States: The Case of Singapore," Chapter 11 in Lino Briguglio and Kisanga, Eliawony: *Economic Vulnerability and Resilience of Small States.* Malta: Formatek Ltd.

Porter, Michael E. (1990). *The Competitive Advantage of Nations.* London: Macmillan.

Quah, Jon S.T. (1998). "Singapore's model of development. Is it transferable?" in Rowen, H.S. (ed.). *Beyond East Asian Growth: The political and social foundations of prosperity*. London: Routledge, pp. 105–25.

Ramirez, Carlos D. and Ling Hui Tan (2004). "Singapore Inc. versus the Private Sector: Are Government-Linked Companies Different?" IMF Staff Papers, Vol. 51, No. 3, pp. 510–28.

Rodan, Gary (1997). "Singapore in 1996," *Asian Survey*, 37, pp. 175–80.

Rodrik, Dani (2004). "Growth Strategies," Mimeo, at http://ksghome.harvard.edu/~drodrik/GrowthStrategies.pdf.

Rodrik, Dani and Arvind Subramanian (2003). "The Primacy of Institutions," *Finance and Development* 40 (2): pp. 31–4.

Rodrik, Dani, Arvind Subramanian, and Francesco Trebbi (2002). "Institutions Rule: The Primacy of Institutions over Integration and Geography in Economic Development," IMF Working Paper 02/189. Washington, DC: International Monetary Fund.

Sachs, Jeffrey (2005). *The End of Poverty: Economic Possibilities for Our Time.* New York: Penguin Group.

Schein, Edgar H. (1996). *Strategic Pragmatism: The Culture of Singapore's Economic Development Board.* Cambridge, Mass.: MIT Press.

Schumpeter, Joseph A. (1947). *Capitalism, Socialism and Democracy*, second edition. New York: Harper.

Seah Chee Meow (1999). "The administrative state: quo vadis?" in Linda Low (ed.), *Singapore: Towards a Developed Status.* Oxford: Oxford University Press.

Sen, Amartya (1999). "Democracy as universal value," *Journal of Democracy* 10.3 (1999), pp. 3–17, at http://muse.jhu.edu/demo/jod/10.3sen.html.

Smith, Adam (1776). *An Inquiry into the Nature and Causes of the Wealth of Nations,* at http://www.econlib.org/library/Smith/smWN.html.

Tan Ling Hui (2003). "Rationing Rules and Outcomes: The Experience of Singapore's Vehicle Quota System," in IMF Staff Papers, Vol. 50, No. 3, pp. 436–57, at http://www.imf.org/external/pubs/ft/staffp/2003/03/pdf/tan.pdf.

Tanzi, Vito (1998). *Corruption around the World: Causes, Consequences, Scope, and Cures*, International Monetary Fund working paper, WP/98/63.

Tay, Richard S. (1996). "Alleviating traffic congestion in Singapore: A review of demand management," in Lim Chong Yah, *Economic Policy Management in Singapore.* Singapore: Addison-Wesley.

Then Yee Thoong. "The National Wages Council and the wage system in Singapore," in Lim Chong Yah et al. "*Wages and Wages Policies: Tripartism in Singapore.*" Singapore: World Scientific Publishing Co. Pte. Ltd.

Transparency International (2005). "Corruption Perceptions Index," at http://www.transparency.org/cpi/2005/cpi2005_infocus.html.

Trocki, Carl A. (2005). *Singapore, Wealth, Power and the Culture of Control.* New York: Routledge, Taylor and Francis Group.

Tsao Yuan (1986), "Sources of growth accounting for the Singapore Economy" in Lim Chong Yah and Peter Lloyd (eds.), *Resources and Growth in Singapore.* Singapore: Oxford University Press.

United States Government, Department of State (2006). Singapore—Country Report on Human Rights Practices, at http://www.State.gov/g/drl/rls/hrpt/2005/61626.htm.

Vogel, Ezra (1989). "A Little Dragon Tamed" in Kernial S. Sandhu and Paul Wheatley (eds.), *Management of Success: The Molding of Modern Singapore.* Singapore: Institute of Southeast Asian Studies, pp. 1049–66.

Weil, David N. (2005). *Economic Growth.* Boston: Pearson Education, Addison-Wesley.

Wilkin, Sam (2004). "Maintaining Singapore's Miracle," August 17, 2004 Editorials *Countryrisk,* at http://www.countryrisk.com/editorials/archives/2004_08_17.html.

Wilson, Woodrow (1887). "The Study of Administration," *Political Science Quarterly,* Vol. 2, No. 1 (June 1887), at http://teachingameriacanhistory.org/library/index.asp?document=465.

Wong, Evelyn S. (2000). "Partnership of trade unions in national development programmes and in promotion of labour mobility in Singapore," Discussion Paper DP/117/2000. Geneva: International Institute for Labor Studies.

World Bank (1993). *The East Asian Miracle: Economic Growth and Public Policy.* New York and Oxford: Oxford University Press for the World Bank.

World Bank (2002). "Building Institutions for Markets," *World Development Report.* New York: Oxford University Press.

World Bank (2005a). "World Development Indicators," Database, at http://devdata.worldbank.org/dataonline/.

World Bank (2005b). "Economic Growth in the 1990s: Learning From a Decade of Reform," Washington, DC: World Bank.

World Economic Forum (2005). *The 2005 Global Competitiveness Report.* UK: Palgrave Macmillan; also at http://www.reforum.org.

World Health Organization (2006). *The World Health Report 2006—Working together for health,* at http://www.who.int/whr/2006.

Wu, Friedrich and Thia Jang Ping (2002). "Total Factor Productivity with Singaporean Characteristics: Adjusting for Impact of Housing Investment and Foreign Workers," *Economic Survey of Singapore,* 3rd Quarter, Ministry of Trade and Industry, Singapore, pp. 45–55.

Young, Alwyn (1992). "A tale of two cities: Factor accumulation and technological change in Hong Kong and Singapore," in Stanley Fischer and Olivier Blanchard (eds.), NBER *Macroeconomics Annual 1992,* No. 7. Cambridge: MIT Press.

Index

G

J

K

R